CHAMPIONSHIP OFFENSE

40 Winning Basketball Strategies From 40 Winning Coaches

Edited by Joe Shinners

Lessiter Publications, Inc. • Brookfield, WI

Publisher's Cataloging-in Publication

(Provided by Quality Books, Inc.)

Championship offense: 40 winning basketball strategies/from 40 winning coaches; Joe Shinners, editor.— 1st ed.

p. cm.
ISBN: 0-944079-29-6

1. Basketball—Offense. 2. Basketball—Coaching.
I. Shinners, Joe

GV889.C43 1998   796.323'2
                                  QBI98-886

Cover photo by NCAA Photos
Cover and book design by Maureen Splitgerber

International Standard Book Number: 0-944079-29-6

Published by Lessiter Publications, Inc.,
P.O. Box 624, Brookfield, WI 53008-0624.
For additional copies or information on other books or publications offered by Lessiter Publications, write to the above address.
Telephone: (800) 645-8455 or (414) 782-4480. Fax: (414) 782-1252.
E-Mail: info@lesspub.com.

Manufactured In The United States of America

Foreword

BASKETBALL COACHES are never satisfied with the level of their teaching skills. They mentally drill themselves by seeking the best information they can find in an effort to add to the foundation of knowledge upon which they are always building.

Championship Offense: 40 Winning Strategies From 40 Winning Coaches represents just one more brick in that foundation. We hope that the decades and decades of information presented in this volume will offer valuable insight to coaches on all levels.

There isn't any one coach who knows everything about the game of basketball, but all coaches have something to offer the game. Here are 40 outstanding contributions from some of the best offensive minds in the game.

— Frank Lessiter
Editor/Publisher
Winning Hoops

KEY TO DIAGRAMS

① Player with the ball   ∿∿➤ Dribble

✕ Defensive Player or   ──➤ Cut
   player in line during
   drill

                                 ──┤ Screen

- - ➤ Pass

Contents

Chapter 1

Fundamentals

Five Key Rules For Effective Passing
By Jeff Lisath, Boys' Assistant Coach, Portsmouth High School, Portsmouth, Ohio

THERE ARE five key rules that form the backbone of a passing game offense: passing, screening, movement, balance and spacing.

Certain ideas in coaching basketball fade into and out of popularity. The concept of the passing game has remained vital.

These ideas are effective with most but not all personnel and do not constitute "rules" that are best in all coaching situations.

PASSING

Passing is the key, but indiscriminate movement of the ball can be self-defeating. You should require that players look for open teammates before passing the ball rather than anticipating a teammate will be open. Also, instruct your players to avoid following their passes, an idea some coaches may feel is somewhat unorthodox.

✗ **PRINCIPLES:** When the ball is passed from the top of the key to the wing, have players screen away from the top and the bottom. When the ball is passed from the wing to the top, have players down screen on both sides.

✗ **DRILLS:** Four-on-four, half-court game in which the offensive team throws a certain number of passes prior to taking a shot.

Five-on-five, half-court game in which the offensive team has 30 seconds to maintain possession of the ball without dribbling or shooting (running passing game). Each violation, such as dribbling, a bad pass, traveling or a turnover, is counted and the team with the fewest violations in a predetermined time period has the pleasure of watching the other team run wind sprints.

SCREENING
✗ **BASIC RULE:** If a defender is in position to be effectively screened, the primary responsibility of the offensive players is to screen that defender. It takes many hours of practice to develop the ability to anticipate these situations; howev-

er, some coaches will find it very well-defined. All screens are designed to free an offensive player moving toward the ball.

X TIPS: It's important to stress that the cutter must wait for the screener to set the screen and move opposite of where the defense is playing the cutter. In the event the defense switches, the screener must open up and turn toward the ball while keeping his or her body between the ball and the defender.

X DRILLS: Two-on-two screening from the "wing to the box" or from the "box to box." Run screens against straight man-to-man and switching defenses.

MOVEMENT

All players must have proper movement to force the defense into situations that will result in good shot opportunities. Movement also keeps all players alert and improves team cohesiveness.

All positions on the court are interchangeable. At times, your big players will be in position at the top with the ball, but the alignment can be effective. Players, regardless of size, should be able to pass, cut and screen.

Unless there is a breakdown, a big player will not have to dribble or shoot from the wing or the top, but will find times when that shot or dribbling opportunity is open.

SPACING

No players should be more than 10 to 15 feet apart and no player should be more than 19 feet from the basket during any possession in the half-court set. This makes it very difficult for the defense to recover because the offense will always be in shooting range after each pass. One defensive breakdown can result in an open shot, many times a layup.

BALANCE

Players must be in position so that the floor is balanced at all times. Position one player at the top, one on each wing, one in the low post and one in the high post as seen in Diagram 1.

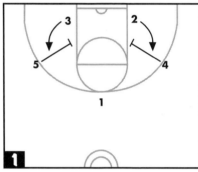

Diagram 1: Passing game set. 4 and 5 start on wings and down screen at the point of attack.

Diagram 2: The ball is passed to the wing with 1 and 4 screening away.

Diagram 3: The ball is passed to the top with 2 and 1 down screening.

Diagram 4: The ball is passed to the left wing. 3 and 1 screen away.

Diagram 5: The ball is passed to the top with 4 and 3 down screening.

Diagram 6: The ball is passed to the left wing with 5 and 4 screening away.

Jeff Lisath has been a long-time boys' assistant coach at Portsmouth High School. He was an assistant coach on the school's state championship team in 1988 and a player on the school's team that won the Ohio State Title in 1978. He also was the head men's coach at Columbus State in Columbus, Ohio, leading the team to a 59-9 record in three years.

The Drive Series
By Rod Kirschner, Boys' Head Coach, Horton High School, Horton, Kan.

BASKETBALL is a game of action and reaction. The player who can cause the defender to react has a decided advantage in quickness, a key weapon in an offensive player's arsenal.

Players have only three options available when they have the ball: pass, dribble and shoot. When players do not have the ball, they have only three options available: clear out an area (cut away), clear themselves (cut to get open for a pass or rebound) and clear a teammate (screen to get a teammate open).

The drive series is predicated upon the purpose of giving players moves for any situation and enabling players to read the defense and take advantage of weaknesses it presents. It is important that players receiving passes square up to the basket as the ball is in flight

so they are in the triple-threat position when the ball is caught.

The triple-threat position allows players to face the basket (square up), be quicker and establish themselves as offensive threats. Players must always pivot on the non-shooting foot (left foot for right-handers and right foot for left-handers). By executing a proper pivot, your players become constant scoring threats because they are properly balanced and in the correct shooting position.

Here are six moves you should drill your players on to improve their offensive effectiveness.

QUICK SHOT

Your players should use the quick shot if the defense is not in proper position when the ball arrives on the square and catch. Emphasize good balance and shooting form in practice as players take time becoming comfortable shooting quickly and properly reading the defense.

JAB FAKE, SHOOT

If a defender closes out on your player's square-and-catch move, then reacts by dropping off on the fake, the offensive player should use this move. Have your players give a short jab with the shooting foot while faking the ball upward. Your players should not bring the ball back down to the waist, but keep the ball at about chest height. After the fake, the ball will be in position to get off a quick shot over the defender.

JAB FAKE, EXPLODE

A layup is the goal of this move. When the defender closes out and does not react to the jab fake, the defender will have the up foot on the slowest side. The defender will have to drop step when the offensive player blows by on that side.

The explode move is made to the offensive player's strong side. After the jab fake, your player should blast the front (shooting) foot forward, trying to get it past the back foot of the defender.

Your player's shoulders should come below the waist of the defender, but the player's chin should be kept up for proper balance. The ball must be dribbled when the shooting foot hits the floor.

The dribble should be low, long and pounded hard for quickness. Your player should continue to dribble in for the layup (or pass to an open player if he or she is picked up by another defender).

JAB FAKE, DRIBBLE, JUMP SHOT

When the defender closes out and doesn't react to the jab fake and takes a long drop step or gets too low while trying to stay with your offensive player, your player should jab fake, explode for one or two dribbles and shoot a jumper. If the defender doesn't react to the jab fake, your player should pull up quickly and shoot a jump shot after one or two dribbles while the defender keeps pace by moving low.

ADD A FAKE REVERSAL

This is another opportunity for a layup. After the jab fake, dribble and hesitation move, your player should fake a reversal and explode to the basket for a layup. Have your player use this move when the defender closes out but does not react to the jab fake and denies the jump shot by maintaining coverage on the explosion move.

After dribbling and recognizing the defender is in proper coverage, your player should use a hesitation dribble by slowing down, faking a reversal by partially turning the body and acting out the reversal. When the defender stops, your player can blast in for a layup.

CROSSOVER FOR LAYUP

When the defender does not react to the jab fake, the up foot of the defender is on the slowest side because he or she will have to drop step when your player makes a move to go by on that side. The crossover move is to your player's off or weak hand.

After the jab fake, your player should swing or snap the ball to their off hand either low and quick over the shoe laces or quickly over their shoulders. They must get the ball to their off hand then blast the front (shooting) foot forward, trying to get it past the back foot of the defender.

Players shoulders should come below the waist of the defender, brushing the inside shoulder against the defender but keeping the chin up for balance. The ball must be dribbled when the shooting foot hits the floor. The dribble should be low, long and pounded hard for quickness.

A player should continue to dribble in for the layup or a pass to an open player must be made if a defender picks up the drive to the hoop.

Remind players to jab fake and step straight ahead on the crossover move. Do not have them loop and give the defender the advantage.

Rod Kirschner has coached high school teams in Kansas, Missouri, Ohio and Kentucky. He has won more than 300 games and 10 conference championships during 26 years of coaching.

Championship Offense

Sideline Out-Of-Bounds Play

This out-of-bounds play is very effective in attacking a man-to-man defense during the last seconds of the game.

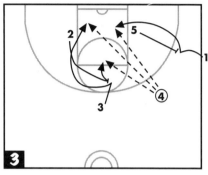

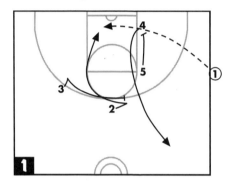

Diagram 1: Player 5 sets a screen for 4 while 3 sets a screen for 2. 1 can pass the ball directly to 2 under the basket.

Diagram 3: 1 comes in and 5 sets a screen for 1. Then 2 sets a screen for 3. 4 can then pass to 1 or 3 or to 2 rolling into the lane.

—**Vinod Vachani,
Welham Girls' High School,
Dehra Dun, India**

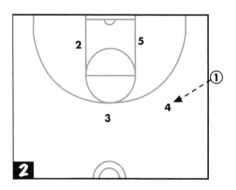

Diagram 2: If 2 isn't open, 1 inbounds to 4.

Chapter 2

Man-To-Man

The "ISO" Movement Offense
By Jeff Barker, Boys' Head Coach, Dunlap High School, Dunlap, Ill.

USE THE MAN-to-man "ISO" Movement Offense to complement your personnel. The setup offers continuity and ensures your best post player will never leave the post area. It also allows the remaining members of the team to enter the post area to score.

It is designed to isolate a dominant player in the post—either a true post player or strong guard.

Transition into the offense can be done from the fast break out of two setups. Most teams use a three-out, two-in or a four-out, one-in alignment. The post player must get to the strong-side low-post area for the offense to begin.

Early in the offense, stress patience and ball reversal to wear down the defense and make penetrating passes and drives easier to execute. Demand that your players read defenders and act accordingly throughout each phase of "ISO" continuity.

The "ISO" offense provides many scoring opportunities for your team if your players execute the fundamentals of screening, cutting, pinning, reading and passing. There are many post triangles formed, two-man game opportunities, chances to penetrate and screening situations that create opportunities to read the defense.

The offense is designed to ensure ball reversal. It also utilizes many concepts of motion offense while providing natural spacing in the three-out, two-in set.

This is the most important attribute of the offense as it allows for fluid adjustments to changing or trapping defenses.

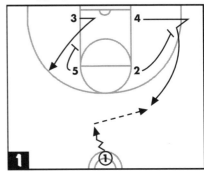

Diagram 1: This is an isolation in

a regular half-court set. 2 and 5 set screens for the cutters, 3 and 4, who read the defenders and cut accordingly.

Diagram 2: The pass has been entered to 4. 2 immediately posts for two counts and screens away for 5, forcing a tough switch for the defense.

The best post player should now be covered by the opposition's shooting guard. 2 posts up for a quick count and back screens for 1, who makes a back cut to the basket.

This "quick" flash will either leave 2 open or cause 2's defender to be in poor help position for the back screen on 1's defender.

The back screen isolates the post player for a two count and allows 2

to roll to the ball off the screen. If 4 feeds 5 in the post, the ball can be dumped to the back cutter.

Diagram 3: 4 reverses to 2 at the top of the key. This also sets up a high-low dump pass if 5 can pin the defender.

Diagram 4: 1 vacates the post to set a back screen for 3. 5 continues to pin the defender.

Diagram 5: 2 reverses the ball to 1. 3 posts for a two count then screens away for 5, who should be isolated in the post.

Diagram 6: 3 completes the series by setting a back pick for 2 and rolling toward the pass. At this moment, 3 is in good position to hit the shot or penetrate the lane if the defense is caught out of position.

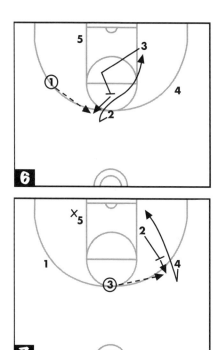

6

7

Diagram 7: 2 screens for 4, who cuts to the basket. 3 reverses to 2 to complete the continuity.

SPECIAL PLAYS

If the offense does break down, go directly to a three-out, two-in motion game. Here are two special plays to run from the set.

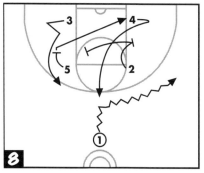

8

Diagram 8: 1 dribbles in to the right as 4 ducks under a screen by 2

and cuts to the top of the key. 2 sets a cross screen for 5, who cuts to the strong-side post. The pass can go to any open player.

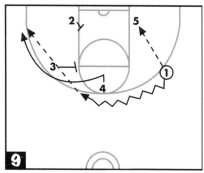

9

Diagram 9: 2 and 3 set a double-screen for 4 as the second option in the opposite corner. The main option is a two-man game between 5 and 1.

Jeff Barker has coached basketball for 11 years, including seven as a boys' head coach at Dunlap High School. He has won more than 100 games and one conference title.

Double-Post Man-To-Man Offense
By Lester King, Boys' Head Coach and Athletic Director, Goodrich High School, Goodrich, Texas

THIS IS a balanced offense that will work successfully on both sides of the court. The point guard has the option of dribbling straight toward 2 and if the point guard does, 2 takes one step in and sets a screen. 4 moves out and sets another screen.

We want our post players to play deep so the defense will play in front of them. Of course, if the defenders don't play in front, just lob the ball to the post players in front of the basket.

A good post player will try to ease out a little and see how far he or she can get with the defense still fronting. If the post player can move the defender out and still hold off the defender, lob over the defender to the post player.

Diagram 1: This is the basic set for the double-post offense. 1 is one step from the head of the circle. 2 and 3 are extended from the free-throw line. 4 and 5, the post play-

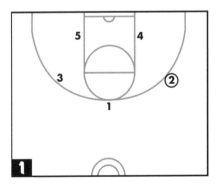

ers, are located along the free-throw lane about 3 feet in front of the backboard.

Diagram 2: The first passing option is 1 to 2. 2 tries to feed 1 as 1 cuts through to screen for 5. You'll notice 4 has moved out parallel to 2 on the first pass. Never pass the ball to the baseline in a man-to-man offense.

Diagram 3: If the first option fails, 2 tries to feed 5 breaking toward the free-throw line.

Diagram 4: If the second option fails, 4 moves up to set a pick for 2, who dribbles toward the baseline as

Championship Offense

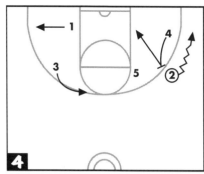

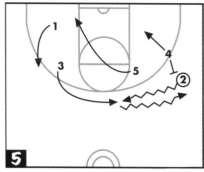

4 breaks back toward the basket. If the defenders switch, 2 feeds 4. If the defenders don't switch, 2 goes to the baseline and takes a shot.

Diagram 5: If 2 does not want to take the pick, he or she should drib-ble toward 3, who will move over and meet 2 at the top of the circle. 3 takes the handoff and continues to dribble toward 4 and the baseline. 4 should screen for 3, opening up a screen and roll back to the basket.

Lester King has been coaching since 1974, leading Goodrich High School to a district title eight consecutive years at one point and a second-place finish in the Texas State Tournament in 1998. He was named Polk County Enterprise East Texas Coach Of The Year four times. King has more than 300 victories in his career.

Double Away Vs. Man Defense
By Keith Siefkes, Boys' Head Coach,
Beth Eden Baptist School, Denver, Colo.

WHEN COACHES must make do with the players who walk through the door, the Double Away Vs. Man Defense can be a key even if you don't have a strong post player. There are five key points to running the offense against a man-to-man defense:

1 On initial guard cuts, passer goes first.

2 Forwards push off inside foot to get open when beginning a cut.

3 The player who is isolated on the weakside must stay wide.

4 Post players must turn to the free-throw line on rolls across the lane to keep the defense honest. Post players must follow the ball.

5 Players cutting off double-screens can go high or low, depending on the defense.

Diagram 1: Ball can be entered to either side of the court.

Diagram 2: Forwards make L-cuts along the lane to get out and open. 2 passes to 4 and cuts to inter-

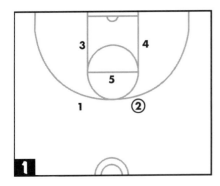

top of the key. 5 rolls to the mid-post ball-side block after 1's cut.

Diagram 3: 4 passes to 3, who passes to 2 out wide. 4 cuts off the double-screen to the low-post ball-side block. (4 can go over or under.) After the screen, 1 switches with 3. 5 rolls toward ball-side block. Positions are now reset as in Diagram 1.

change with 3 (passer always goes first). 1 pushes off opposite foot and cuts off 2 and 5 on the way to the ball-side block. 3 replaces 2 at the

Keith Siefkes has coached basketball for 21 years, including 17 in Minnesota where he won two conference titles. Siefkes is in his second year at Beth Eden Baptist School in Denver, Colo.

Man-To-Man Continuity Offense
By Dave Nordeng, Boys' Head Coach,
Laconia High School, Rosendale, Wis.

THIS MAN-TO-MAN continuity offense offers a strictly run pattern offense that teaches many concepts of a motion offense.

With this offense, the weakside defenders are occupied during the post ups of 5 and 4, making for an easy entry pass.

Diagram 1: Start in a double stack. Both 2 and 3 break out. When 2 re-

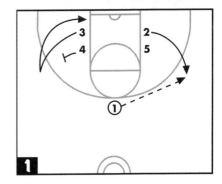

       Championship Offense

ceives the pass, 4 back screens for
3.

Diagram 2: 1 sets a down screen
for 3. 5 posts up. 2 passes to 3.

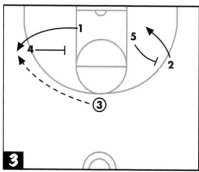

Diagram 3: 5 sets a back screen
for 2. 4 sets a down screen for 1. 3
passes to 1.

Diagram 4: 4 posts up. 3 down
screens for 2. 2 cuts out to
receive the pass from 1. Continuity continues.

Diagram 5: As a variation, 4 and 5
set cross screens for 1 and 3,
respectively. 2 passes to 3 on the
wing for the a three-point shot.

Diagram 6: With 4 or 5 on the
wing, the ball can be passed back
inside to post up a guard. 2 sets a
screen for 1, who comes out to
reset the offense if the play fails.

*David Nordeng has coached boys and
girls basketball for 11 years at Laconia
High School in Rosendale, Wis.*

QUICK HITTER

Inbounds Play

Diagram 1: Against a zone defense, 5 screens nearest defender to get inside position on the weakside block. 3 cuts to the ballside corner. 2 backs up and acts as a safety release outside the three-point line. 4, your best leaper, circles and goes down the lane toward the ball.

Diagram 2: Against a man-to-man defense, the cuts are the same except for 5, who sets a diagonal back screen for 4, then rolls down to the weakside box. 4 must wait for the screen to get open.

—**Teresa C. Bentley,**
Jenkins High School,
Jenkins, Ky.

Chapter 3

Zone

Iowa Zone Offense
By Pat Fischer, Boys' Head Coach,
Holy Angels School, Sidney, Ohio

THE IOWA zone offense can be run against any zone defense, eliminating the need to adjust to changing defenses.

The keys to the offense are:
- ✔ There is always a player in backside rebounding position.
- ✔ Players can specialize with certain skills emphasized in each position.
- ✔ There are many opportunities to get the ball inside for a basket.
- ✔ It can be run to either side with a continuous pattern.
- ✔ Options and special plays are built in to keep the defense off balance.
- ✔ Your best shooter is always positioned for the open jump shot.
- ✔ Your best post player can be isolated in a one-on-one situation.

PERSONNEL AND ALIGNMENT

1: Point guard. Must be a good ballhandler and passer. Should always be conscious of gap penetration and getting the ball inside to any open post player.

2: Best outside shooting guard. Must be able to consistently hit the jump shot and must always be in a shooting position, especially against a sagging defense.

3: Small forward or wing player. Must be able to hit the baseline jumper and pass the ball inside.

4: Best outside shooting guard. Average rebounder who must be able to hit the jump shot from the wing area. Positions self on the block opposite the ball and is always conscious of working for position on the backside for offensive boards.

5: Best athlete and post player. Must be able to play with back to the basket. Doesn't need great size but must be an inside scoring threat at all times.

Diagram 1: 1 should attack the zone from the side approaching the basket in a straight line. As 1 approaches, 3 pops to the corner and 5 slides up the lane while

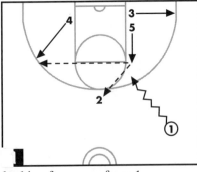

looking for a pass from 1.

If the defense plays behind 5, 1 can pass to 5 for the shot. If the defense sags to help out on 5, 5 should look to 2 at the top of the key or to 4 breaking to a weakside wing position.

Diagram 2: If 5 does not receive the ball in the high-post area because the defense fronts in the post, 1 passes to 3 in the corner. 3 must be a scoring threat. 5 seals and

rolls low to the ball-side block for the baseline bounce pass from 3.

Diagram 3: If 5 does not receive the pass, 3 reverses the ball to 1 and cuts across the baseline to the opposite corner. 1 should look inside to 5 posting on the block. If the play to 5 is not there, 1 reverses to 2. 4 pops out to a wing position and 2 reverses the ball to 4. On each reversal pass, the receiver must be a scoring threat.

Diagram 4: When receiving the ball on the wing, 4 should always be conscious of the skip pass to 1. 5 posts up on the block. 1 looks inside to 5 posting up.

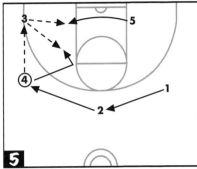

Diagram 5: If 4 does not throw the skip pass to 1, the pass should go to 3 in the corner. 4 should begin a cut through the zone to the opposite

block, but turn and face the ball in a high-post position. 5 cuts to the ball-side block and establishes post-up position. This is a high-low situation. 3 should look to pass to 4 and 5.

Diagram 6: If 4 and 5 do not get the ball, 4 continues through the zone to the opposite block. 3 reverses the ball to 2 to establish continuity.

Diagram 7: After passing the ball to 2, 3 runs the baseline to the opposite corner. 2 reverses to 1. On the pass from 2 to 1, 4 pops to a wing position and 1 reverses the ball to 4. On each reversal pass, the receiver must be a scoring threat.

Diagram 8: 4 passes to 3 in the corner and begins to cut through the zone to the opposite block. At the elbow, 4 should turn and face the

ball in the a high-post position. 5 cuts to the ball-side block and establishes a post-up position. This represents a high-low situation in which 3 should be looking to feed 4 and 5. 1 replaces 4 and 2 replaces 1.

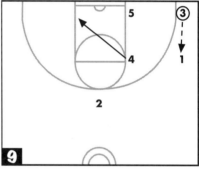

Diagram 9: If 4 and 5 don't get the ball, 4 continues through the zone to the opposite block. 3 reverses the ball to 1 and continuity is established.

Diagram 10: In Diagram 2, if it's determined that 5 is being fronted or played on the baseline side, 5 should seal the defender. 3 reverses the ball to 1, who reverses the ball to 2. 2 passes inside to 5 rolling across the lane. Stress a bounce pass in this situation.

ZONE OFFENSE GENERAL PRINCIPLES

⊗ The point guard must aggressively attack the zone and always look for gap penetration.
⊗ Players must crash the backside offensive boards.
⊗ Always be conscious of gap penetration. Make the defense commit and then dump the ball off to the open player.
⊗ Always be conscious of inside players, but make sure players can hit the perimeter jump shot.
⊗ Whenever the ball is in the corner, always be conscious of the baseline bounce pass into the post when the post player is being played on the high side.
⊗ Always recognize opportunities for the skip pass.
⊗ Use ball fakes to move the zone.
⊗ Use special plays to keep the defense honest and off balance.

Pat Fischer has been coaching youth basketball for the past nine years.

"Five-Up" Secondary Break
By Kevin Sivils, Boys' Head Coach, Runnels High School, Baton Rouge, La.

USE THIS secondary break or offensive entry against a zone defense. This has been effective against aggressive 2-3 or 2-1-2 zones.

Diagram 1: This is the basic alignment as the players run the floor on the secondary break. Run a numbered fast break to fill these spots.

Diagram 2: Line up in a 1-4 high alignment to attack a set zone defense. This usually works after a dead ball.

Diagram 3: 5 sets a solid screen on the defensive guard to the right of 1. 3 cuts underneath the zone to the short-post area, or about 15 feet from the goal and slightly behind it. 2 spots up for a three-point shot, and 4 seals the defensive center if possible. 5 cuts to the weakside rebounding position after the screen.

Diagram 4: It's not unusual for 1 to have a good 15-foot jump shot coming off the screen. After 1 has penetrated the zone to the elbow area, the defense has three players to defend four offensive players. 4 usually is the team's best scorer and first scoring option. The defense will try to play high on 4 and stay on 2. This leaves 3 open on the baseline. If 3 does not have a shot and 4 has sealed the defend-

er on the high side, the pass from 3 to 4 for a layup is an easy one.

Diagram 5: If the defense collapses off 2 to stop the 1-3 or 1-3-4 plays, this leaves 2 with a wide-open three-point shot. Often, teams will close out long or run at 2, leaving the easy pass to 3 on the baseline. Once 3 has the ball on the baseline, the same set of options as described in Diagram 4 are available.

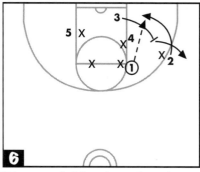

Diagram 6: 3 has the option of back screening the defender who is shadowing 2. 2 fills the spot on the baseline and the same set of options is available. If 3 is a good three-point shooter, this is an effective way to free the player. After 3 screens, the three-point shot is available on the step out to the perimeter as the defense collapses on 2.

Diagram 7: This shows how the play is executed from the 1-4 alignment. Instead of screening for

1, 5 screens for defensive center. 1 hits 4 coming across the lane. If 1 can't make that pass, the pass could go to 2 while 1 is moving up into the zone's seam. 2 can then hit 4 or 3 cutting across the lane.

Kevin Sivils has been coaching boys and girls basketball at Runnels High School for 13 years. His overall record is 307-203. He led the boys team to three conference titles, four district championships and has been named league Coach Of The Year eight times.

Single Read Out Of Box Set
By Mark Cisco, Head Shooting Instructor, Sports City U, Huntington, W.Va.

Diagram 1: 5 and 4 interchange with a flat screen. 3 feints to the middle of the lane and relocates around the three-point line. 2 passes to 3. 1 floats to the point and receives pass from 3. 3 cuts off 4's elbow run for a backdoor lob. 1 reads the single pick and makes a decision to throw the lob pass. If it's not there, 1 looks for 2 coming

off 5's pick for a short wing jumper.

KEY POINTS
✔ This puts the team in a 1-2-2 set with the point guard having the ball in the "see" position.
✔ If 2 shoots, there is backside rebounding help.
✔ The set teaches players to read single screens.
✔ Against the zone, 2 will hold and delay the cut off 5's screen.
✔ 3 has the opportunity for an exciting dunk.

Mark Cisco is in his fourth year as a shooting instructor for youth basketball players at Sports City U, a basketball camp in Huntington, W.Va.

QUICK HITTER

Last Shot Against Zone

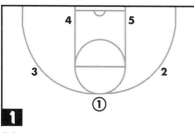

Diagram 1: Initial setup is the 1-2-2 and the ball is moved around until only 15 seconds remain in the game. Then the call is made to run the play. Attack inside first, unlike many zone theories. Make sure the shot is taken with 6 seconds left.

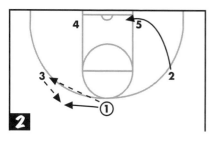

Diagram 2: 1 passes to 3 and goes toward the pass to create a lane for 3's return pass. 2, the best shooter, stacks under 5.

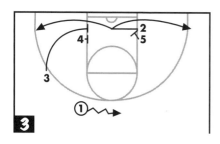

Diagram 3: 3 sets a second screen below 4. 1 dribbles to the middle of the court and reads 2's cut. 2 comes out off 5's screen or the double-screen set by 3 and 4.

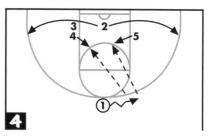

Diagram 4: 1's first look is to 4 or 5 on a flash after 2 clears their screens. The second look is the shooter. The player who comes off 2's side—4 or 5—flashes to the middle. The final option is 2's jump shot or a jump pass into 4 or 5 in the post.

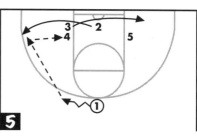

Diagram 5: If 1 passes to 2 coming off the double-screen, 3 clears to the opposite side. 3 clears because there is a double-team on the weakside and 4 has the post position alone.

—Pat Sullivan,
College Of St. Francis,
Joliet, Ill.

Chapter 4

Motion

Balanced Motion Offense
By Mark Starns, Video Coordinator, Boston Celtics, Boston, Mass.

THIS BALANCED Motion Offense involves all five players by opening opportunities for three-point shots and inside shots from the block. All players need to work on three-point shooting, post-up moves at the block or medium post, ball handling and individual moves.

Spacing is important if you are looking for three-point shots because the three-point shot will open up the inside game. The triple-stack entry is used if you don't have

a fast-break opportunity. If you are fast breaking, get into the set seen in Diagram 2, which represents a combination of UCLA high-post moves and motion offense.

Diagram 1: This shows the entry from the triple stack. 1 comes across the 10-second line. 3 flashes to the wing. 2 flashes to the top of the key.

Diagram 2: 1 passes to 3. 1 runs the defender off a back screen by 5. 1 posts the defender at the

block. 2 screens down for 4. 4 replaces 2.

Diagram 3: 3 passes to 4. 2 flashes to the free-throw line extended. 4 passes to 2. 3 runs the defender into 5's screen. 1 replaces 3.

Diagram 4: If 3 doesn't get the ball, 4 screens down on 5. Rotation continues.

Diagram 5: 2 passes to 5. 2 screens down on 3. 3 replaces 2. 2 posts up.

Diagram 6: If 3 doesn't get the ball, rotation continues as 5 reverses the ball to 1.

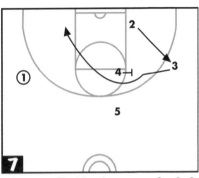

Diagram 7: 4 back screens for 3. 3 cuts high off the screen. 3 posts up at the block. 2 replaces 3.

Diagram 8: If 3 doesn't get the ball, 5 screens down on 4. 4 replaces 5.

Diagram 9: 1 passes to 4. 1 screens down on 3. 1 posts up at the block.

Diagram 10: If 3 doesn't get the ball, rotation continues. 4 passes to 2.

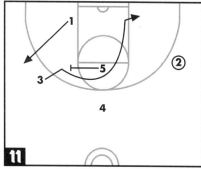

Diagram 11: 5 back screens for 3. 3 posts up at the block. 1 replaces 3. Rotation continues.

QUICK HITTERS OFF THE MOTION OFFENSE

"1 UP"

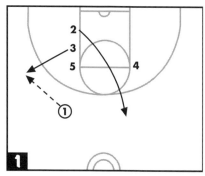

Diagram 1: 3 flashes out. 2 breaks to the top of the key. 1 passes to 3.

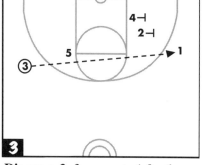

Diagram 3: 3 passes to 1 for the three-point shot or the best available shot off the staggered screen by 4 and 2.

Diagram 2: 1 rubs his or her defender into 5's back screen. 4 and 2 screen down. 1 curls.

"3 DOWN"

Diagram 1: Same rotation employed as in "1 Up." After 3 passes to 1, 5 back screens for 3. 3 runs the defender into the screen.

Diagram 2: 1 passes to 3 for the inside shot.

"4 DOWN"

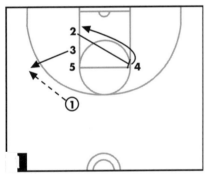

Diagram 1: 3 flashes out. 1 passes to 3. 2 back screens for 4. 4 drop steps the left leg to pin the defender on 2's screen. 4 curls hard to the block.

Diagram 2: 3 hits 4 with a pass for the shot down low.

"35 PICK AND ROLL"

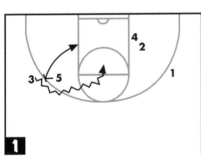

Diagram 1: Run "1 Up" play. 3 and 5 work together. 3 dribbles defender into 5's screen, then rolls to the basket. 3 can shoot or pass to 5 for the shot.

Mark Starns coached high school basketball in Kentucky for eight years before joining the Boston Celtics of the National Basketball Association.

Single-Post Continuity Offense
By Bob Rhodin, Boys' Head Coach,
Fletcher High School, Neptune Beach, Fla.

THE SINGLE-Post Continuity Offense is a motion offense designed to create mismatches and get the ball inside to the post. The post player moves from block to block and is screened each time by a different teammate.

The offense also provides great rebounding balance, screen-the-screener action and outside shot opportunities on the ball reversal. The offense works well against man-to-man and zone defenses.

ENTRY PASS

Diagram 1: 1 passes to 2 and cuts to the opposite box. 5 is posting up. 2 can pass to 5 in the post or to 4, who has V-cut to get open at the top of the key.

Diagram 2: 2 passes to 4. 5 ducks in. 4 can pass to 5. If 4 can't pass to 5, 4 dribbles toward 3 as a key to set up a screen. 3 screens for 1. 4 passes to 1. 1 can shoot the open jump shot.

Diagram 3: After screening for 1, 3 screens for 5. 5 must cut low off all cross screens (screen-the-screener action). 1 can pass to 3 or 5 for an open shot.

Diagram 4: If the jump shots are

not open, 1 looks to pass to 5 in the post. If the pass to 5 is not open, 1 passes to 3, who dribbles toward 2 (key to screen). 2 screens for 4 and 5 then pops out to the top of the key. 4 follows 2 out to the top of the screen to receive 3's pass for the open jump shot from the wing.

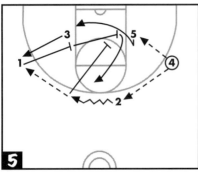

Diagram 5: 5 always cuts toward the baseline off screens, such as this cut off 1's screen. 3 screens for 2 (screen-the-screener action). 4 passes to 5 or 2. 2 dribbles toward 1. 1 screens for 3. 2 passes to 3.

CONTINUITY CONTINUES

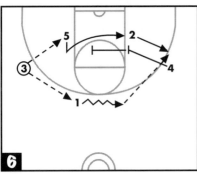

Diagram 6: 3 can pass to 5 down low or reverse the ball to 1 to continue continuity. 4 screens for 2 cutting to the wing, then for 5 cutting to the baseline toward the opposite

block. 1 passes to 2 at the wing.

CAROLINA ENTRY

Diagram 7: 1 passes to 4. 5 ducks in. 4 looks to pass to 5. 4 passes to 3. 5 seals the defender and pivots to the block. 3 passes to 5.

Diagram 8: 1 sets a back pick for 4. 4 cuts to the basket. 3 can pass to 5 posting up, to 4 coming off the back pick or to 1.

Diagram 9: 3 passes to 1. 1 looks to pass to 5, then dribbles at 2. 2 screens for 4. Continuity is set.

DRIBBLE ENTRY

Diagram 10: 1 dribbles to the wing. 2 clears to the weakside post. 5 back screens for 4. 1 can pass to 4 in the post or to 5 stepping out after the screen.

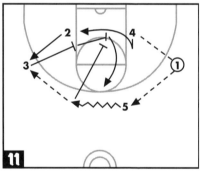

Diagram 11: 1 passes to 5. 5 can take the shot or dribble toward 3. 3 screens for 2 and 4. The continuity continues.

Bob Rhodin coached boys and girls basketball for more than 18 years at Fletcher High School, compiling an overall record of 312-146 and winning five Florida Gateway Conference titles. He currently coaches youth basketball.

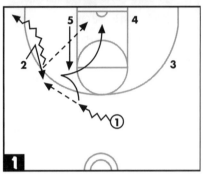

Diagram 1: 1 must choose a side to trigger the correct post player to move up to the high-post area. If the left side is chosen, 5 comes high. 2 fakes in and comes back for the pass then dribbles toward the corner. 1 cuts off 5's move. 1 looks for the pass from 2. If the pass to 1 isn't there, 2 continues into the corner.

receive a pass for the jump shot or looks to pass to 4 inside on 4's duck into the lane. In this case, 1 flares to the corner.

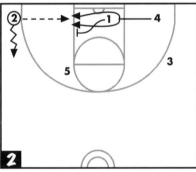

Diagram 2: If the pass can't go to 1, 1 screens for 4. 4 cuts or posts in position to receive a pass from 2. 2 can bring the ball back out top to reset the offense.

Diagram 3: If 5's defender helps out on 1's cut, 5 steps back to

Diagram 4: If there is no help from 5's defender, 1 continues to screen for 4. If 4 is not open after a brief post up, 4 continues to the corner. 1 stops on the box. 5 sets a pick and roll with 2. 2 dribbles right and can pass to 4 out wide in the corner, to 3 or use 3's screen to drive to the basket.

Diagram 5: 2 can drive to the basket or look for 5 on the roll. 2 also has the option to pass to 4 in the

Diagram 7: If nothing develops, 5 sets pick and roll with 1 or 2. 1 can take the jump shot at the free-throw line. 3 down screens for 4. 1 can pass to 4 coming off the screen or to 3 rolling toward the hoop after the screen for 4.

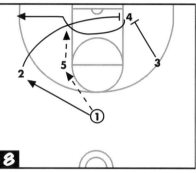

Diagram 8: Here is the setup for the backdoor cut. 1 goes to 5. 2 goes backdoor and 1 takes 2's spot. If 2 does not receive the pass, 2 picks for 4, who hooks into the lane. If 4 doesn't receive the pass, 4 cuts through to the corner to set up a passing triangle.

corner if 4's defender helps on the pick and roll. 3 screens down for 1. 2 can pass to 3 after the screen or to 1 moving to the wing off 3's screen.

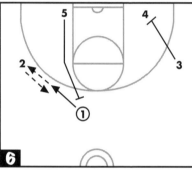

Diagram 6: This is the bump play. 1 chooses a side and passes to the corresponding wing player. 1 tries to cut off 5's screen. 2 passes back to 1. On any bump play, there is an automatic screen down on the opposite side, shown, here as 3 screening for 4.

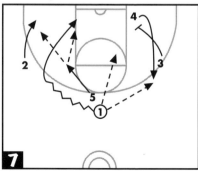

Nate Webber has coached high school and college level teams. Webber led McCorristin High School's boys team to New Jersey's Trentonian League title in 1998, when he was named the league's Coach Of The Year. He also previously coached the men's team at Kean College in Union, N.J. He played at Elizabethtown College in Elizabethtown, Pa.

Sideline Play For A "3" Or An Inside Shot

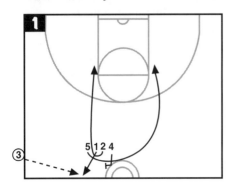

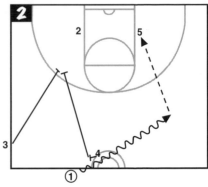

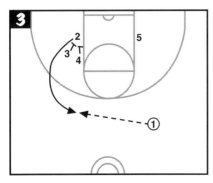

Diagram 1: We line up in a straight line directly in front of the ball. 5 runs a loop to the basket and then posts up. As 5 passes 1 and 2, 2 circles in front of 1 and posts up. 1 pops out as 2 crosses in front of him or her. 4 steps out and sets a high screen.

Diagram 2: 1 gets a pass from 3 and dribbles off a high screen by 4. As 1 comes off 4's screen, you look inside for 5 on a post-up.

Diagram 3: As 1 dribbles off the high screen, 3 and 4 move down to set a staggered double-screen for 2. 2 uses the staggered screen and looks for a three-point shot.

Diagram 4: If a three-point shot is not available, 3 pops out and 4 posts up.

—**Tom Moriarty,
Oneonta H.S.
Oneonta, N.Y.**

Chapter 5

Fast Break

Fast Break For All Situations
By "Doc" Zinke, Boys' Head Coach,
McClintock High School, Tempe, Ariz.

TRY TO RUN the fast break after a missed shot, a made shot, a missed foul shot or after a steal.

A fast break should be organized with players assigned certain spots or positions. The fast break can demoralize a team that cannot defend it and stop the opposition

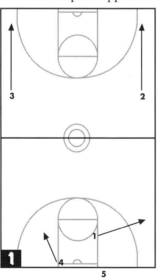

from scoring. Players and fans enjoy this type of basketball. Players, however, must be in top-notch shape to run the offense effectively.

BASIC SETUP
Diagram 1: Here is the base formation for the fast break. 1 is the point guard and primary ballhandler. 2 and 3 are wing players who are good shooters and can get down the floor fast. 4 is the quickest big player and a strong rebounder who trails the play. 5 is the outlet player and the slowest big player on the floor.

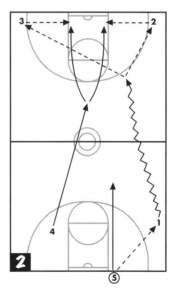

Diagram 2: 5 releases the outlet

pass to 1, who is positioned at the free-throw line extended. 1 immediately dribbles up the court looking to pass to 2 or 3, both of whom are positioned at the baseline. If the outlet pass is made to 1, 4 becomes the trailer on the ball side of the wing receiving the inbounds pass. 2 or 3 look for jumpers or a pass to 4 trailing on the play. 5 moves toward half-court as the safety.

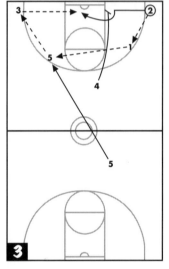

Diagram 3: This is a second option. If 2 cannot hit the trailer with the pass, reverse the ball from 2 to 1 to 5 to 3 with 4 setting a low screen for 2. 2 drags down and

"Doc" Zinke has coached basketball for the past 31 years, 18 of which he has been coaching the boys program at McClintock High School. Zinke led McClintock to the Arizona State Title in 1986 when he was named the Arizona Coach Of The Year. McClintock has been in the state playoffs five out of the last 10 years. His overall coaching record is 470-330.

comes off 4's screen and receives a pass from 3. 4 rolls to the basket. The offense is now in position to run the flex offense if a score off the reversal is not possible.

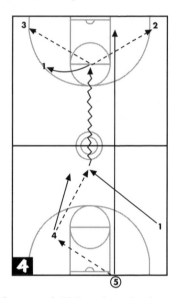

Diagram 4: If 5 can't make the outlet pass to 1, the ball should be released to 4 as the safety option. 1 cuts into the middle of the court to receive the pass from 4. 1 dribbles to the key, making a pass to either 2 or 3. After making a baseline pass, 1 clears to the opposite side to allow the trailer a ball-side lane. 5 then becomes the trailer and 4 becomes the safety outlet.

DRILLS
4-Man Continuous Break
Diagram 5: 4 throws the ball to 3 by banking it off the backboard. 3 jumps up, grabs the ball and turns outside to make the outlet pass to 1. 1 immediately passes to 2 in the

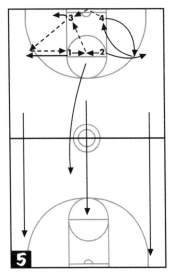

middle while 4 breaks out to fill the lane. 2 passes to 3. 3 banks the ball over to 4, who has returned to the low post. 4 turns and makes the outlet pass to 2, who passes to 1 in the middle. 3 fills the opposite lane.

12-Man Continuous Break

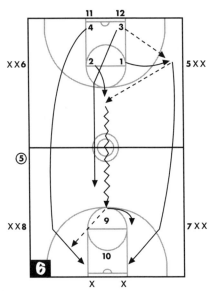

Diagram 6: 3 passes to 1. 1 passes

to 2 cutting into the middle. 2 dribbles down the middle of the court with 1 and 4 filling the outside lanes. 3 becomes the trailer in the four-man break. 9 and 10 form a defensive tandem. As soon as 9 or 10 rebound or a shot is made, they send the outlet pass to 7 or 8, and the break continues to the opposite end of the court, where 11 and 12 now form a defensive tandem.

This is a good drill to get big players involved in the break and to work on options within the break, such as wing shots, guard curls and trailers. Run this every day.

Break Off Made Free Throw

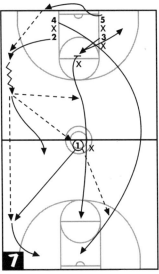

Diagram 7: 5 makes the outlet pass to 2. 4 goes to the opposite lane. 1 goes to the side of the outlet pass. 2 turns and dribbles while looking for a long pass to 4, 1 or 3. 2 becomes the trailer and 5 is the safety release.

Four-Out Perimeter-Oriented Secondary Break

By Chuck Carringer, Boys' Head Coach, Oak Ridge High School, Oak Ridge, Tenn.

THE FOUR-OUT Perimeter-Oriented Secondary Break is designed to provide transition scoring opportunities. There are several reasons why a secondary break should be an integral part of an offense, especially the four-out break.

- The offense offers consistency. Look to run your secondary break after all opponent scores and misses unless your team has a numerical advantage. It is possible to run only the secondary break on opponent scores or misses but not both.

- The secondary break brings organization to the offense. All players must understand their responsibilities.

Here are the players' lane assignments after opponents score a basket:

1: Receives inbounds pass as far up the court as possible, usually on the side of the basket the player will be attacking.

2: Right lane.

3: Left lane.

4: Inbounds the ball and fills the vacant spot on the break opposite 1.

5: Runs to the rim for a quick score, then moves to the weakside low-post position.

Here are the lane assignments after opponents miss a shot:

1: Seeks the ball for an outlet pass.

2 & 3: Fill the most convenient outside lanes. Do not assign lanes after a miss.

4 & 5: First post player down the floor goes to the rim, then moves to the weakside low-post position. The second player down the floor fills the vacant top position, most likely opposite 1. At times after misses, 2 or 3 will handle the ball and 1 will assume the remaining role. If you only have one true post player, allow that player to fill the low-post position.

Here are some key advantages of the offense.

- The offense takes advantage of quick scoring opportunities before the defense is completely set.

- Turnovers will be reduced. Your best ballhandler will control the basketball 90 percent of the time.

- This alignment allows players who can penetrate the option to drive to the basket.

- Three-point shots will open up on the ball reversal and screening action.

- Inside scoring can be attempted after the ball reversal.

- Spreading out the defense gives

the offense better opportunities to grab offensive rebounds.

■ Great spacing and floor balance are afforded.

■ The offense can be easily adjusted to fit personnel.

PROPER ADVANCEMENT

After gaining possession of the ball, the offense must determine if it should run a primary break, secondary break or a set offense.

If the offense has a numerical advantage or is in a one-on-one or two-on-two situation, a primary break is the best option. If it's a dead-ball situation, run a set offense. All other situations should be considered your secondary-break opportunities.

Have the point guard handle the ball. Rebounders should clear the rebound to the point guard, who seeks possession of the ball. The ball can be advanced down the middle of the court or either sideline.

Encourage passes up the floor if the receiver is in an advantageous situation. Occasionally, another player will advance the ball if there is a long rebound or steal that did not result in a primary break.

Allow certain post players to take one or two "bust out" dribbles before making the outlet pass.

1 should always look just below the rim while advancing the ball to maintain vision of the entire court and probe the defense for penetration opportunities that could lead to a high-percentage drive to the bas-

ket, a dump-off pass to an awaiting post player or a kick out for a three-point shot.

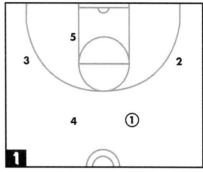

Diagram 1: Once the ball has been advanced into the front court, the offense takes a four-out alignment.

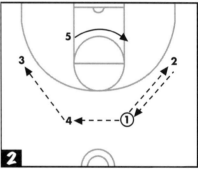

Diagram 2: If 1 cannot penetrate, the pass goes to 2 to shift the defense and allow 2 an opportunity to penetrate on the cleared side. If 2 penetrates on the baseline, 5 moves to the dotted line to open a better passing angle.

1 could pass to 4 to start the reversal or skip pass to 3. 5 must remain on the opposite side of the ball. This alignment provides off-side rebounding, sets up the ball reversal and allows for penetration by perimeter players.

OFFENSIVE SEQUENCE

Within their limitations and restrictions, each player's offensive sequence should be:

- Shoot.
- Penetrate.
- Reverse the ball.

Diagram 3: When the ball is completely reversed to 3, there are two possible offensive actions.

First, 2 flex cuts off 5's screen. 5 then flashes to the ball-side high-post position off a staggered screen by 1 and 4. 1 and 4 come back out top.

Diagram 4: 2 cuts off staggered screens by 1 and 4. 5 cuts to the ball-side low-post position if 2 chooses this option. This isolates 5 in the post. 1 and 4 set up with proper spacing after setting their screens. 4 dives to the open block

if he or she is a true post player or has the option to move into space along the perimeter if guarded.

OPTIONS OFF BREAK

At this point, the offense has concluded the secondary break and enters either a motion or set offense.

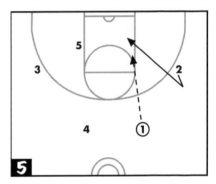

Diagrams 5 and 6: When facing tough defensive pressure that makes ball movement difficult, take advantage of spacing by not fighting pressure and executing backdoor cuts. Pick a signal, such as a pass fake, as a call to execute a backdoor cut.

CLEAR OUT

Diagram 7: Call for this clear-out play with a hand signal or sign. 1

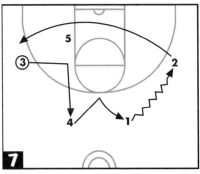

7

dribbles to the wing. 2 clears to the opposite side. 3 and 4 rotate up one position. 1 now has an opportunity to utilize the flex or staggered screens when the ball is reversed.

POST A WING

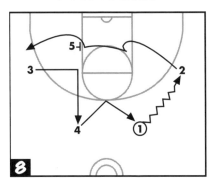

8

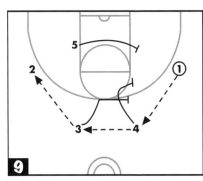

9

Diagrams 8 and 9: 1 dribbles to the wing. 2 appears to clear to the other side but instead seals the defender

for a post-up opportunity. 3 and 4 rotate up one position. 2 posts up for 2 seconds then clears to the opposite side. 5 screens for 2 and takes a position opposite the ball. 2 looks for the high-low pass from 4 on the reverse from 1. Scoring action on the ball reversal remains the same.

POINT GUARD PASS, CUT, POST

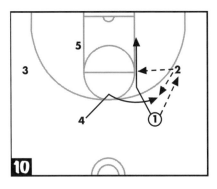

10

11

Diagrams 10 and 11: This play is cued with 1 cutting to the basket after passing to 2, who immediately looks for the return pass to 1. 1 can post up for 2 seconds before clearing to the other side. 3 and 4 rotate up one position. 5 pops out and provides a cross screen for 1. 5 moves opposite the ball.

SCREEN ON BALL

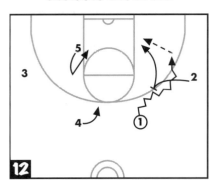

Diagrams 12 and 13: 1 directs 2 to set a screen. 1 comes off 2's screen while looking to penetrate. 1 must take two dribbles off the screen for spacing purposes. 2 may roll to the basket (Diagram 12) or step back for a potential three-point shot (Diagram 13). 3, 4 and 5 remain spotted up but are alert to flashing to the open area if their defender rotates. At this point, you are in the motion offense.

Diagram 14: 1 directs 4 to set a screen. 1 comes off the screen by 4 and looks for penetration. 1 must take two dribbles to ensure spacing. 4 may roll to the basket with 5 moving to the other side.

Diagram 15: Another option has 4 step back and set up a possible three-point shot. 2 and 3 set the appropriate spacing. 2 slides along the perimeter toward the action. 3 fades closer to the baseline.

LOB, STEP OUT, POST

Diagram 16: 1 passes to 2, who returns the pass. If this pass or any other pass is denied, utilize pressure

release options. 1 passes to 4. 5 continues to post up without changing sides as is normally the case.

Diagram 17: After screening, 2 pops out to receive a pass from 4. 2 looks for a possible three-point shot. If 2 is not open for the shot, he or she should dribble to the wing area to improve the passing angle to 1 posting up.

Diagram 18: 1 posts for 2 seconds, then sets a cross screen for 5. 1 slides off screen by 4. This action works well against switching defenses. In sequence, 2 looks for 1 posting up, 5 off the screen and 1 again off the down screen by 4.

SLICE CUT

Diagram 19: 1 passes to 2 then screens for 4, who can simply flash

to the ball-side low post. 2 looks for 4 cutting to the block. 1 screens for 3 coming to the ball. 1 spaces appropriately after screening. This motion results in a layup for 4.

BACKDOOR ATTACK

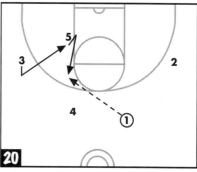

Diagram 20: 1 passes to 5 just above the weakside elbow. 3 immediately cuts to the backdoor looking for a pass from 5.

Diagram 21: 4 fills the wing area vacated by 3. 1 screens for 2 to occupy the defense and give 5 the opportunity to drive to the basket.

THREE-POINT SHOT OFF FLARE

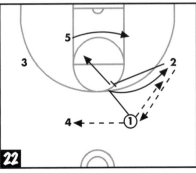

Diagram 22: 1 passes to 2, who returns the pass to 1. 1 reverses to 4. 2 sets a flare screen for 1. 4 looks for 1 flaring for a three-point shot or 2 cutting to the basket. If 1 and 2 are covered, 4 reverses the ball to 3.

ATTACKING ZONES

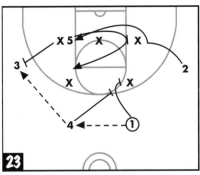

Diagrams 23 and 24: Run the same action against zone defenses as you do against man-to-man defenses. Proper spacing provides opportunities to penetrate into the gaps of the

zone. 5 looks to screen on the weakside for possible skip passes. In this example, either 1 or 2 could skip pass to 3 in the flex cut, as shown in Diagram 23, or the staggered screen, as shown in Diagram 24. Both create difficult situations for the zone to defend.

Chuck Carringer is a nine-year coaching veteran with an overall record of 160-86. His team won the Tennessee AAA District four times during his tenure. Carringer was named District Coach Of The Year in 1991 and 1993.

Option To Finish Off Break

By Dan Schinzel, Boys' Head Coach,
Omaha Westside High School, Omaha, Neb.

WHEN NOTHING is available early in the break, ball reversal using 5 as the trailer initiates options at the end of the fast break.

The following description assumes the early break has been initiated on the right side of the floor. Everything can be mirrored if the ball is brought up the left side of the floor.

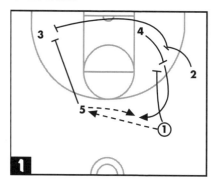

Diagram 1: This movement can be employed after the ball is reversed to 5. Instead of coming up the lane looking for a pass from the top, 4 sets a back screen for 2.

This initiates a series of flex cuts. 2 screens down for 4, who receives a pass from 5. 2 back screens for 3 and receives a down screen from 5.

This action exploits defenses that overplay the perimeter. Teams that have a 4 who can shoot the perimeter jumper will find that player open on the first down screen.

Dan Schinzel has been coaching basketball for nine years, three as a head coach.

QUICK HITTER

Inbound Vs. 2-3 Zone

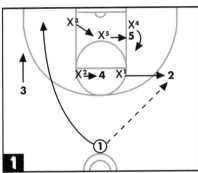

Diagram 1: This play is designed to create a mismatch for your perimeter player who has the ability to finish near the basket. Begin in a 1-3-1 look with 1 passing to 2 at the wing. 1 moves to the corner on the weakside. 2 must catch the ball above the free-throw line. X1 will move out to guard 2. 3 moves into position below the free-throw line.

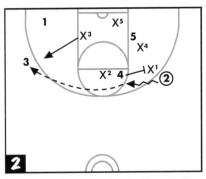

Diagram 2: 2 goes hard off the ball screen by 4. 2 passes to 3. 2 can pass to 1 if X3 cheats.

Diagram 3: 3 has three options: hit 1 isolated against X5 in the short corner, pass to 4 diving to the block if X5 cheats to cover 1 or pass to 5 in the mid-post for a jump shot or dump down to 4.

Adjustments: You can have 2 or 3 slide down to the short corner and 1 slide to the wing on the initial pass.

—**Ricky Norris,**
Oak Ridge High School,
Oak Ridge, Tenn.

Chapter 6

Flex

Disguises Improve Flex Production
By Sid Rodriguez, Boys' Head Coach,
Ridgeway High School, Ridgeway, Mo.

THE FLEX offense, which fades in and out of popularity, is a powerful and effective offense when properly disguised. By disguising your flex offense, easy scoring opportunities will open up and your opponents will be driven crazy.

Here are two entries into the flex, both of which offer high-powered scoring opportunities. The offense can be run out of a high-low double-stack set and a 1-3-1 set. Also, the more traditional 2-3 set can be used but is not shown.

Following are six key reasons for using the flex with the traditional 2-3 and other entries:

1 Offers different look than opponents are used to seeing.

2 Leads to easy scoring opportunities with proper execution.

3 Allows for creativity in a structured offense.

4 Creates constant visual problems for the defense.

5 Suited for a team with one or two solid offensive players and a group of role players. All players must be able to set good screens and shoot a layup or short jump shot.

6 Puts a premium on good ball-handling skills to succeed.

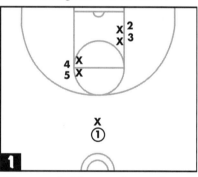

Diagram 1: The opening set is shown in the high-low double stack.

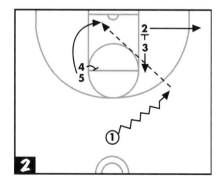

Diagram 2: 1 dribbles toward the wing area opposite 5. 2 pops out to the three-point area. 3 slides up the lane to draw the defender away from the basket. 4 back picks for 5, who rolls to the basket for the 1-to-5 backdoor lob.

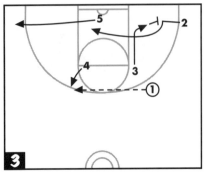

Diagram 3: If the backdoor lob does not develop, enter into the flex. 3 slides down the lane into a post position. When 5 sees the lob is not coming, 5 moves out to the three-point area to clear for the cutter.

4 steps out to the three-point area to receive the 1-to-4 reversal pass. 2 runs the baseline and cuts off 3's screen. Now the offense is in the 2-3 flex.

1-3-1 SET

In the 1-3-1 set, always look for a quick hitter either off a drive by 1 or a backdoor pass and layup (or dunk!).

Sid Rodriguez coached high school boys and girls basketball teams in Missouri for 15 years, compiling a combined record of 409-306. He won numerous conference and district titles and was named Kaysinger Conference Coach Of The Year in 1992 after leading his team to the title.

Diagram 4: This is the setup for the 1-3-1.

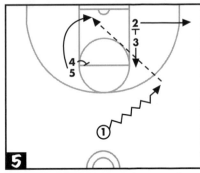

Diagram 5: 3 screens down to free 2, who pops out to the three-point area. 3 steps away from the lane to keep the defender away from the basket. 5 steps out and sets a high screen for 1. 1 can drive to the basket and beat the defense for a layup or pass to 5 moving to the basket.

Diagram 6: This is the beginning

    Championship Offense

of the flex movement. Either reverse the ball to 4, who has faded to the weakside elbow, or 4 screens down to bring up 5 for the pass reversal. When the ball is reversed, the 2-3 flex movement begins.

QUICK HITTER

A Quick "3"

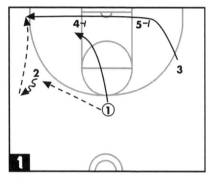

Diagram 1: 1 passes to 2 and goes to set a double-screen with 4. 2 dribbles out and then turns to hit 3 coming off a screen by 5 and then the double-screen.

Diagram 2: This play can also be used to get the ball to the post. 4 screens across for 5 and 1 breaks across to the opposite wing. 3 can take the three-pointer, hit 5 coming across or swing the ball around to 1 via 2 for the weakside shot.

—Tammy Hedspeth,
St. Gertrude High School,
Richmond, Va.

Chapter 7

Shuffle

The Shuffle Revisited
By Steve Sorensen, Boys' Assistant Coach, Boulder High School, Boulder, Colo.

WHEN I BEGAN looking at different offenses, I identified eight basic premises I wanted to target.

I wanted the offense to incorporate:

✦ Continuity.

✦ Cutters moving to the basket to attack and avoid standing around on the perimeter.

✦ Passing game principles.

✦ Passers having at lease two, ideally three, places to pass the ball at all times.

✦ Flexibility to allow variety based on strengths of personnel, or to allow more structure if players lacked the ability to pick up options out of the offense.

✦ Court balance.

✦ A rebounding triangle formed when any shot is taken.

✦ The ability to easily insert set plays into the offense for specific game situations.

I settled on the shuffle offense, but decided on the shuffle out of a 1-3-1 set. The shuffle positions are first cutter, second cutter, feeder, point and post.

BASIC SHUFFLE

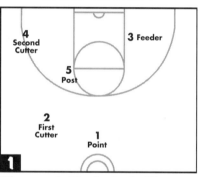

Diagram 1: The basic shuffle as taught by then-Air Force Academy head coach Bob Spear and his assistant Dean Smith begins with an overloaded 2-1-2 set.

Diagram 2: As 2 passes to 1, 3 breaks out to receive the ball.

Diagram 3: When the ball is passed from 1 to 3, 5 sets a pick for 2, who cuts to the basket looking to receive a pass for a layup or short jump shot.

Diagram 4: If the pass to 2 cannot be made, 2 should cut to the ball-side corner. 5 sets a second pick for 4, who breaks to the ball.

Diagram 5: The rotation is completed when 1 sets a back pick for 5

coming out to the top of the free-throw circle. 5 is looking to take a jump shot or to reverse the ball.

Diagram 6: Each player is now in position to run the shuffle to the other side. 3 dribbles out to become the first cutter, 5 becomes the point, 1 becomes the feeder, 4 is at the post position and 2 is the second cutter.

SCORING OPPORTUNITIES

Notice that there are four scoring opportunities in the basic shuffle movement.

✦ When 3 first receives the ball, the first look is to take a quick drive to the basket or take a short jump shot where the ball is caught. The cutters from the opposite side time their cuts properly so 3 has time to make the decision to drive or shoot.

✦ The second scoring option has 2 cutting across the lane and receiving the ball either for a layup or to get fouled in the process of driving to the hoop.

✦ The third scoring option sees 4 cut across the lane for the mid-range jumper.

✦ Finally, 5 is usually open at the top of the free-throw circle for a long two-point or three-point attempt.

A DIFFERENT ANGLE

The 1-3-1 set is utilized because it has high- and low-post options, a decent power game and brings flexibility to the shuffle.

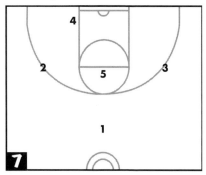

Diagram 7: Tilt the positions on the court from a 2-1-2 set to the 1-3-1 and run the same picks and cuts as in the basic shuffle.

Diagram 8: 1 passes to 3. 2 cuts off 5's pick. If 2 doesn't get the ball on the cut, 2 posts up on the strong side and asks for the ball. 2 should have a short jump shot or jump hook shot.

Diagram 9: 5 then sets a pick for 4. 4 comes to the strong-side high post. 2 goes to the low post.

Diagram 10: 1 picks for 5 on the screen-the-screener play. 5 moves to the point position after 1 rolls to the weakside and sets the pick.

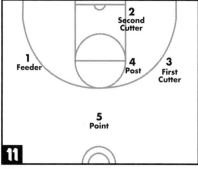

Diagram 11: Players are now in position to run the shuffle to the other side.

KEY COACHING TIPS

Several coaching points must be emphasized when using the 1-3-1 set. Just as you teach your players to set up their defenders when using a screen, you must emphasize the importance of this concept to the first and second cutters.

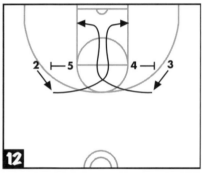

Diagram 12: Tell the first cutter to take one step away from the basket before making the cut off the post player.

This gives a better angle for the shuffle cut and makes the defense think the cutter is going to replace the point player.

Tell the first cutter to stay in the middle of the lane so the entire ball side of the lane is open if the pass is received.

Diagram 13: This shows the proper angle a post player uses to set a screen for the second cutter coming off the weakside block. The second cutter also makes a step away from the basket.

Again, this fools the defense into believing the offensive player is going somewhere else, opening up the lane for the first cutter.

Diagram 14: The only exception to this rule is when the second cutter is a strong power player who can score over the top of the defense.

In this case, we tell the second cutter to stay on the block when the pick comes and roll around the screen for a close-range shot.

Steve Sorensen has coached basketball for more than 20 years. He is an assistant coach for News Release Basketball, an athletic ministry that takes teams to play in Europe.

Inbounds "Spread"

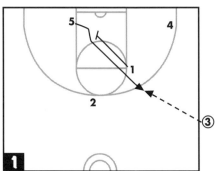

Diagram 1: 3 inbounds to 5 after 1 down screens for 5.

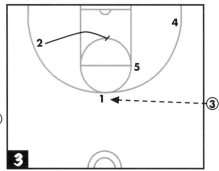

Diagram 3: 3 can also inbound to 1 for a three-point shot.

Diagram 2: After 5 catches the pass, 4 up screens for 3 to create a scoring opportunity. 2 screens the screener, 1. 2 pops out.

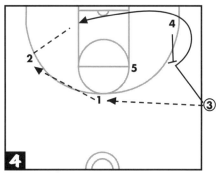

Diagram 4: 1 reverses the ball to 2, who hits 3 for the flex cut.

—**Myron Lowery**
Harding University High School,
Charlotte, N.C.

Chapter 8

Triangle

Triangle "O" Vs. 2-3 Zone
By Mike Beck, Boys' Head Coach,
Groveport Madison High School, Groveport, Ohio

THE CHICAGO BULLS made the Triangle Offense popular and complex. Simplifying it shows the pure passing angles and offensive opportunities important to every team.

I have used this offense and it has been very effective for both our high school boys and girls teams. The perimeter players put a lot of pressure on the defense by looking to score as all players should do at all times.

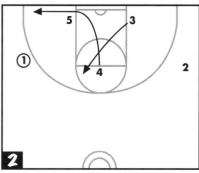

At this point, send 4 below the zone on the baseline and have 5 pin the bottom defender.

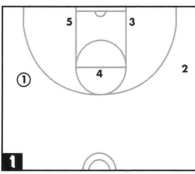

Diagram 1: Initial set is a 3-2 vs. a 2-3 zone. Perimeter players are spread out with no specific order to the triangle.

Diagram 2: 1 brings the ball below the free-throw line extended. Force the top guard in the zone to cover 1.

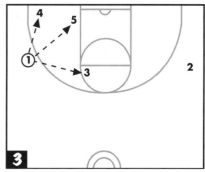

Diagram 3: After 4 vacates to the baseline, 3 replaces 4. Many times this is wide-open because the defenders' heads begin to turn to see what the offense is doing.

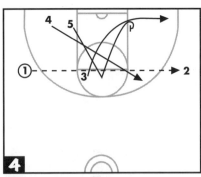

Diagram 4: This setup produces the most opportunities to score. The skip pass to 2 will reverse the ball.

3 sets the pin and post isolation on the cut. 5 follows and looks high. If nothing is there, 5 follows to the baseline and 4 comes to the high post. This continued reversal puts a great deal of pressure on the zone to adjust and results in easy scoring opportunities.

Mike Beck has been coaching boys and girls for the more than 10 years, including three at Groveport Madison High School.

QUICK HITTER

Play With 5 Seconds Remaining

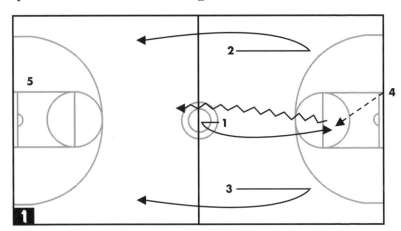

Diagram 1: 4 takes the ball out. 1 fakes long, then comes back for the ball. 2 and 3 fake toward the ball, then break long.

If 4 hits 1, 1 dribbles up the middle of the court looking to pass.

If 4 hits 2 or 3, they should look to center the ball and run the lanes.

5 waits until the ball is across midcourt, then tries to flash into the lane.

—**Mack McCarthy,
Virginia Commonwealth University,
Richmond, Va.**

Chapter 9

Press

Beating A 1-2-1-1 Full-Court Press Defense
By Tim Tolzda, Head Boys' Basketball Coach,
Marietta High School, Marietta, Ohio

THIS PRESS offense has worked on a consistent basis during my career as a head coach.

ALIGNMENT

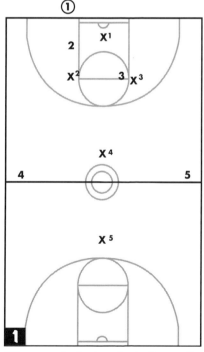

Diagram 1: 1 takes the ball out of bounds. 2 and 3 set up at the low

block and opposite the high elbow, respectively. 4 and 5 set up wide at half-court.

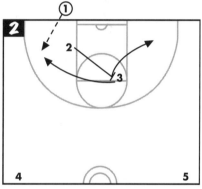

Diagram 2: 2 sets a diagonal screen for 3. 2 moves to the opposite corner for entry. Try to get the ball to 3 because it is a shorter pass on the ball side of the formation.

Tim Tolzda has been coaching basketball for nine years, posting an overall record of 137-59. He has led Marietta High School to four Southeast Ohio Athletic League titles.

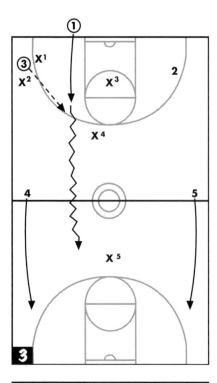

OPTION NO. 1

Diagram 3: As the ball is entered to 3, 1 cuts through the outside of the lane area. 3 tries to get the ball back to 1. If this happens, 4 and 5 fill the lanes looking at a three-on-one situation.

OPTION NO. 2

Diagram 4: If 1 does not receive the ball, 1 goes to the ball-side sideline and waits. When 5 sees this happen, 5 should flash to the ball. 3 will pass to 5.

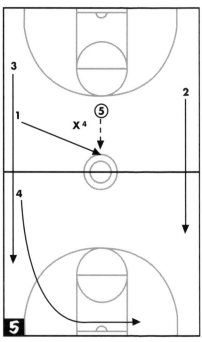

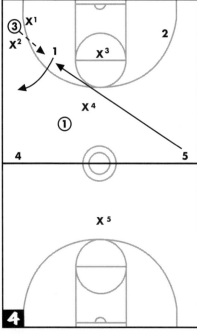

Diagram 5: 5 passes to 1 in the middle. 2 and 3 fill the lanes and 4 releases to the opposite block. This is another three-on-one situation.

OPTION NO. 3

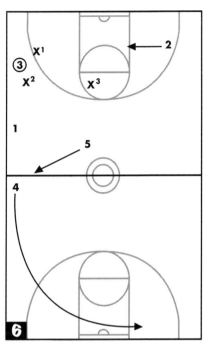

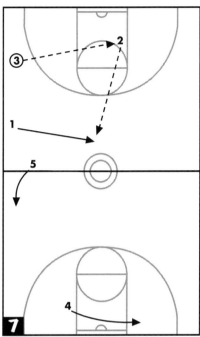

Diagram 6: If 5 does not get the ball, 5 should clear 4 out to the opposite block. 1 holds position.

Diagram 7: 3 reverses to 2, who hits 1 coming back to the middle of the court to set up the three-on-one break.

Chapter 10

Special Situations

Delay Game With Option To Score
By Willie J. Banks, Boys' Head Coach,
Francis W. Parker High School, Chicago, Ill.

EVERY TEAM needs a delay game that is efficient and allows the offense to hold it without turning the ball over in crunch time.

Two sets—stack and split—teach players how to correctly read the defense and make appropriate cuts to the basket.

STACK

In the stack, players run their lanes with 1 keeping the dribble alive until a jump stop is made just inside the three-point line. 1 should never stop at the top of the key. Movement should be on the right or the left of the key.

Use the stack set when the defense is sagging on inside players. The two post players line up first with the wings behind them at the free-throw line extended.

Willie J. Banks played for Illinois-Chicago from 1984 to 1988. He has been a basketball coach for 10 years, posting a 46-36 record at Francis W. Parker as the boys' head coach the past four years.

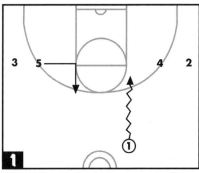

Diagram 1: 4 and 2 are stacked together on the right and 5 and 3 are stacked on the left.

Diagram 2: 5 runs to the "L" and reads the defender. 5 then cuts on a 90-degree angle and receives a pass from 1. 5 should reach for the ball with the right arm extended and

plant with the right foot.

One key is to plant with the proper foot so the offensive player can square up to the basket. When players work the backdoor cut, they should put a fist up instead of opening their hand for effective visual communication with teammates.

1 cuts on an angle to the opposite block looking for the ball with his or her right hand. 4 cuts through after 1 crosses the free-throw line. 5 passes to 4.

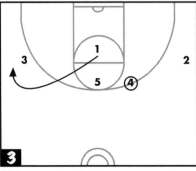

Diagram 3: If 1 does not receive the pass, 1 should run out and fill the spot behind 3.

Diagram 4: 3 steps out to receive 4's pass. The play continues after rotation, but this time with 4 in 1's initial position. Look for the best pass not the quickest pass. Take as

much time as needed off the clock to find the best shot as long as a solid scoring opportunity is found and exploited.

SPLIT

The split series should be used when the defense is playing tight man-to-man coverage.

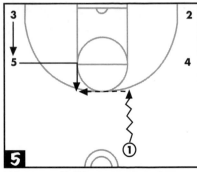

Diagram 5: The two wing players drop down to the corners.1 dribbles in and passes to 5 on the L-cut.

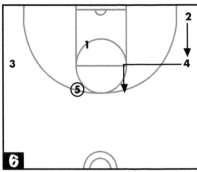

Diagram 6: The wings take the place of the post players when they run to the "L."

Diagram 7: 5 passes to 4 after 4's cut. 5 cuts through to the post and out to the corner. 3 follows 5's initial cut.

Diagram 8: 4 and 3 try a backdoor cut as 5 and 2 cut in from the wings.

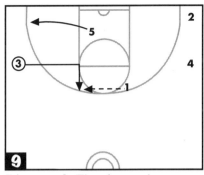

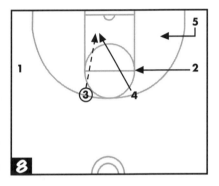

Diagram 9: The player who passes the ball cuts across the free-throw lane and fills the corner. If the player cuts to the backdoor and does not receive the ball, the play will return to the same side but in the corner.

This is a nice delay game, especially for teams who do not have good ballhandlers or great athletes.

Weakside Action Offense
By Bill Wenning, Boys' Head Coach,
Cushing Academy, Ashburnham, Mass.

MOST COACHES have been in a situation where their team has less talent than the opposition.

The Weakside Action Offense is primarily a perimeter-oriented offense designed to create scoring opportunities by playing two-on-two basketball on one side of the court while exposing opportunities on the weakside of the court.

The success of the offense depends on the ability of players to read the defense and execute the pick-and-roll play. The offense emphasizes only inside screens from the area extended from the foul line.

As players become proficient at screening, they learn to use the opponent's contact to help their pivot to the basket to beat the defensive switch. Big players can also step back off the screen, fake the screen and cut to the basket or fade to the wing. Those options are based on how the defense is playing and the offensive skills of the big players.

KEY POINTS FOR FORWARDS SETTING SCREENS

✗ Run up to teammates' defenders and stop at the proper angle.
✗ Keep knees slightly bent.
✗ Keep feet shoulder width apart.
✗ Brush chest against defenders' shoulder.
✗ Anticipate defensive pressure and counteract by keeping a low center of gravity.

CONTINUITY

Diagram 1: To initiate the offense, start in a box set. 4 and 5 down screen. 2 and 3 pop up to the free-throw line extended.

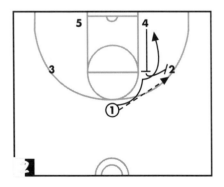

Diagram 2: The offense can be started on either side of the floor. 1 passes to 2. 4 sets a screen off of which 1 shuffle cuts. 4 goes to screen 2.

Diagram 3: After making the shuffle cut, 1 moves to the bottom of the stack on the weakside. 2 and 4 run a pick-and-roll play. 2's options are to take the jump shot, penetrate to the basket and make the help-side defenders collapse around the drive or pass to the screener. 2 cuts to the opposite post position.

Diagram 4: As 2 comes off the screen, 3 down screens for 1. 1 is also an option for 2 coming off the pick-and-roll play.

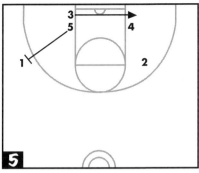

Diagram 5: On the pass to 1, 3 goes to the bottom of the stack on the opposite side. 5 comes up and screens 1's man and the offense is back in the initial set.

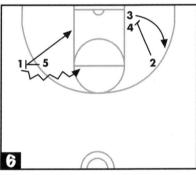

Diagram 6: 1 comes off 5's screen looking for options. 2 screens down for 3 with 4 coming up, setting a second screen for 3. 2 moves to the bottom of the stack on the opposite side.

The continuity of the offense is simple and takes little time to put in. It's the pick-and-roll play that must be practiced at length by all players so their correct movement can be executed precisely and instinctively.

4's and 5's responsibilities are fairly simple. If the ball is on their side of the floor, they must come up hard to screen in the two-man game.

If the ball is on the opposite side, they move on top of the stack, looking for a pass on guard penetration.

Ball-side guards must be patient and allow the big players to set the screen. On the weakside, guards are either on the bottom of the stack receiving a screen or at the free-throw line extended setting a down screen.

The offense can be used to free your best player to create a shot or use penetration to set up a teammate for a shot. The offense can also be used to slow the game down. The more the ball moves from side to side, the wider the middle becomes.

Bill Wenning has coached basketball for 18 years, 13 of which he has spent as the boys' head coach at Cushing Academy. He has more than 200 victories and coached his team to the New England Class B State Tournament Title in 1992, 1995 and 1996.

Weave For Three

By Lason Perkins, Boys' Assistant Coach, Cary High School, Cary, N.C.

AT SOME POINT during the season, you'll find your team in a situation where you need a three-point shot. Most of the time, teams defend the best shooter by playing tight defense to eliminate an open shot.

A good way to loosen up a tight man-to-man defense is to either penetrate to the basket or get a three-point shot by incorporating the weave into one set play.

This set play can be used in special situations during the final minutes of a game when you're trying to play "catch up."

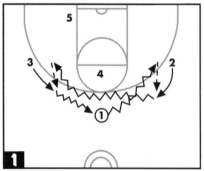

Diagram 1: In starting the weave, 1 dribbles toward 2. 2 comes around to take a handoff from 1. 2 dribbles toward 3, who takes the handoff from 2. 3 dribbles back toward the middle of the floor.

When executing the weave, have players dribble at the defender guarding the receiver of the exchange. If the defense does not

switch in this situation, the player receiving the handoff should have a quick three-point shot opportunity off the dribble.

If the defense switches or the defender is able to recover to guard the offensive player, move the ball to the other side of the floor and continue the weave pattern.

By running the weave one time, the defense is forced to loosen its coverage of perimeter players or is forced into an unwanted switch. Now is the perfect time to run a set play designed to create either a drive to the basket or an open three-point shot.

Diagram 2: 3 dribbles toward 1. 1 comes around 3 for a handoff. As 3 and 1 make the handoff, 4 steps out from the high post and sets up behind the three-point arc to set a ball screen for 1. 5, who has been in the low post, moves across the floor to open a lane to the basket. 1 uses the ball screen by 4 and drives

to the basket. The defender guarding 2 must make a decision. If 2's defender stays on 2, 1 can drive to the basket for a layup. However, if 2's defender drops off to stop 1 from driving, 1 can pitch out to 2 for a three-point attempt.

Another option for 1 is to pass to 5 if 5's defender moves up to stop the penetration.

OPTIONS

Diagram 3: If 2's defender helps on penetration, 2 can step behind 1 when 1 drives to the basket.

This is called "European 3" because many international teams create three-point shot attempts by stepping behind a teammate to create the opportunity to shoot. 1 executes a jump stop, makes a reverse pivot and pitches out to 2. 2 shoots the three-pointer.

If 4 is capable of shooting from three-point range, 4 can step back toward 1. 1 can pass to 4 for the three-pointer.

Diagram 4: It's important that when 4 sets a screen for 1, it is set above the three-point arc.

This action puts 4 behind the arc when receiving the pass from 1.

Diagram 5: If a three-point attempt is a necessity, rather than run the weave, move into position from a 1-4 alignment. 4 steps out to set the screen for 1 at the top of the key. 5 slides into the lane to the low-post area. 1 drives off the screen and looks for either 2, 4 or the open three-point attempt after the initial screen by 4.

Lason Perkins has been an assistant boys' coach at Cary High School since 1993. He previously was a student assistant at Northwestern State in Natchitoches, La.

IN TODAY'S fast-paced, high-pressure game of basketball, a team must have many weapons in its arsenal. Chief among these weapons is the ability to get a three-point shot whenever the team needs one. In order to do this, your team must possess capable and effective guards who understand whom the best three-point shooters are and where "hot" players are at any time.

With this principle in mind, these three plays are designed to produce a three-point shot out of a two-guard set.

PLAY NO. 1

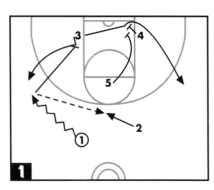

Diagram 1: This play is designed to get a three-point shot for 3. The play is keyed by the point guard dribbling at 3, for whom the play is designed. As 1 gets to the wing area, 3 cuts to the middle of the floor, approximately 6 to 8 feet off

the top of the key.

1 reverses to 2 and sets a down screen for 3. At the same time, 5 moves down the lane to set a double-screen with 4. With the ball at the top of the key, 3 is free to read the defender and either cut off the down screen set by 1 or cut off the double-screen by 4 and 5.

2 should hold the ball out top and wait for 3 to cut. 3 must cut quickly to avoid the 5-second call on 2.

PLAY NO. 2

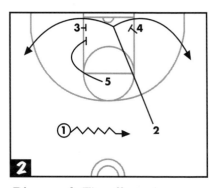

Diagram 2: The offense has decided to set up a play for a guard, in this case 2. This play is keyed by 1 dribbling at 2, the player for whom the play is run. As 1 starts to dribble at 2, 2 immediately cuts to the basket. At the same time, 5 cuts opposite of the cutting guard so as not to interfere with 2's cut.

5 sets a double-screen with the

off-side player, in this case 3. 4 is situated along on the ball side and immediately turns and faces the basket to set a screen for 2. It is important that 4 "head hunt" for 2's defender as 2 moves around the screen.

2 has the opportunity to read the defender and choose the proper screening situation. 2 may cut off the double-screen by 5 and 3 or cut off the screen by 4.

PLAY NO. 3

This play differs from the first two in that there is no predetermined shooter. The guards must use screens wisely and look for the three-point shot or the open player.

Diagram 3: 1 dribbles at the off-side guard. It is important that a verbal call be made to avoid confusing the No. 3 Play for the No. 2 Play.

After hearing the No. 3 call, 2 cuts behind the dribbler in a weave fashion. At the same time, 5 and 4 slide to the three-point line above the elbow area to set a double-screen. 1 hands off to 2 and fades behind the double-screen of 5 and 4.

Diagram 4: As 2 starts to dribble to the other wing, 3 cuts up to screen 2. 2 now has three options: a pass to 1 fading behind the double-screen, a three-point shot after dribbling off the screen or a pass to 3 in shooting position outside the screen.

This play has much merit in that it is hard to scout and offers many options for the three-point shot.

Kenneth Edwards has been coaching at Cox High School in Virginia Beach, Va., since 1993, compiling a record of 103-35. He was named District Coach Of The Year in 1993 and 1994 and coached his team to the Beach District Championship in 1994, 1997 and 1998.

Inbounding With Jam, Jelly and Toast
By Bill Kunze, Boys' Head Coach,
Duluth East High School, Duluth, Minn.

JAM

Diagram 1: 1 screens 5's defender. 4 down screens to the middle. 3 screens the top player. 2 cuts behind the wall of screens for a shot. 5 passes to 2 and hustles to rebound.

JELLY

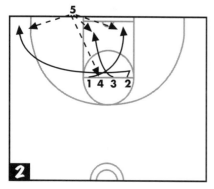

Diagram 2: 2 cuts to the ball-side corner. 1 cuts down the opposite lane. 3 cuts down the lane toward the ball. 4 remains on the foul line where an open shot should result. 5 takes the best shooting opportunity available out of 1, 2, 3 and 4.

TOAST

Diagram 3: 3 steps back for the pass from 5, using picks from 1, 4 and 2. If the play is covered, 3 yells, "Burnt," and 1 cuts to the corner on the ball side. 2 cuts to the corner away from the ball. 4 cuts down the middle of the lane for the pass. 5 hits the open player.

Bill Kunze has been coaching basketball for 25 years, during which he has won two Lake Superior Conference titles at Duluth East and five Camden Conference titles at his previous position at Balaton High School in Balaton, Minn. He has amassed a record of 217-200.

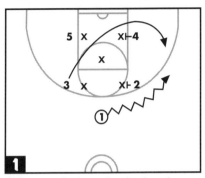

Diagram 1: 1 can begin the play by dribbling left or right. 3 cuts through the lane under 4 and moves close to the wing position.

Diagram 2: 1 can shoot or pass to 3 or lob inside to 4. 3 can step back for the three-point shot, take the open 12-foot jump shot or pass to 4. 2 pops to the top to maintain court balance. 5 cuts up to the elbow to take 2's position.

Diagram 3: In this high-post swing play, 1 passes to 5, who flashed to the high post. 2 circles to the weakside. 3 runs the baseline. 4 flashes to the hoop. 1 moves back to the point.

Diagram 4: 1 ball fakes to the corner and passes to 2, who kicks out top to receive the pass. 3 changes direction and moves off 5's screen. 4 flashes to the high post. 2 dribbles weakside to hit 3, 5 or 4 with a pass.

Diagram 5: If X1 and X2 overplay on the outside, 2 and 3 set inside screens for 1, who drives for a shot from the foul line.

Art Shapiro has coached high school basketball players in a recreation league at Mittelman Jewish Community Center for the past six years. Previously, he was the head boys' coach at Grover Cleveland High School in Ridgeway, N.Y., for two years and at Martin Van Buren High School in Queens, N.Y., for eight years. He played from 1972 to 1974 at the State University of New York at New Paltz.

Last Shot: Make It Count
By Dean Hollingsworth, Boys' Head Coach, Rockdale High School, Rockdale, Texas

HERE ARE key tips to building the confidence of players as they set out to properly execute a game-winning shot.

BE PREPARED

Preparation develops confidence. There are enough problems to worry about at the end of a game, especially when it comes time to run a play with the game on the line. The best way to develop confidence is to prepare for such situations by having a play your team has continually practiced and executed in games.

If a play has worked before, players believe it will work again. They will focus on the task at hand instead of the possible outcome. Most times, players accomplish their goal and win the game.

DRILL PROPERLY

Many coaches spend very limited amounts of time working on special situations. If you have a team that always plays close games, spend more time on winning at the buzzer. If the play for the last shot is part of every offensive drill, your players will soon become very good at it and realize it is important to the team's success.

The amount of time that is needed to go over a game-winning play will be reduced each practice as they get better.

KEEP CLOCK RUNNING

Don't call a timeout before a game-winning play. Timeouts cause problems, such as losing continuity, increasing mental pressure, increasing the pressure on the offense, etc. Momentum can change if a play is stopped.

If the offense has the ball and needs a basket, it will do just as well, if not better, by being prepared for the situation and continuing play. When a timeout is called during play, the coach may be perceived as expressing a lack of confidence in the team's ability to win the game.

It seems the harmful choices outweigh the positive choices when a timeout is called.

MULTIPLE OPTIONS

A last-second play with multiple options is your best choice. Not every coach has a player like Michael Jordan on the roster waiting to win the game.

If you have a proven game-winner on the roster, everyone in the gymnasium knows who will get the ball in crunch time.

Create a play that allows each of your players the opportunity to win the game. All players will work harder at making the play work and feel like they, too, have a chance at winning the game.

MAKE CHANGES

The last-second play that was used last year may not be as effective this year because a key player who can shoot the three-point shot may have graduated or a monster post player no long roams the lane.

Design a play that makes all players feel like they have a chance to contribute if the first option doesn't work. This builds each player's confidence so if the situation arises, they will think you believe in them.

OUT-OF-BOUNDS PLAY

If you call a timeout during a dead-ball situation, you'll need a last-second out-of-bounds play.

The hardest person to guard is the player that takes the ball out of bounds. Here is an example of a proven game-winner.

Diagram 1: 1 picks for 2. 3 passes to 2. 2 passes to 4, who can take the three-point shot. 5 picks for 3. 4 passes to 3 for a layup. 1 and 5 spot up on the three-point line as secondary options after the shot has been taken. Rebounders should kick the ball out to the perimeter to those players.

Dean Hollingsworth has been the head boys' basketball coach at Magnolia High School in Magnolia, Texas, for the last three years. He has coached for 14 years, during which he has won one Texas 3A state title, been named coach of the year four times and compiled an overall record of 237-135.

One-On-One Husky Set
By Jimmy Trotter, Boys' Head Coach,
Hirschi High School, Wichita Falls, TX

THIS IS a half-court continuous offense that works well with strong one-on-one players and produces multiple passing options.

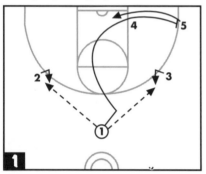

Diagram 1: 1 passes to 2 or 3 (pass determines next option), then cuts through to pick for 5.

Diagram 2: 1 passes to 3 after 3's V-cut. 5 screens for 4 and posts up on the block. 1 cuts through looking for the ball.

Diagram 3: 1 and 4 set picks for 5 as 5 flashes to the low post. 4 immediately flashes to the high post.

Diagram 4: 4 comes off 5's screen to the corner. 2 comes off 1's screen to the free-throw line.

Diagram 5: 1 screens for 3. 3 flashes to the free-throw line.

Championship Offense

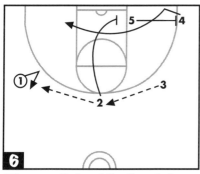

Diagram 6: 4 and 5 roll to their respective starting positions to establish continuity.

Jimmy Trotter has coached basketball on all levels for the past 18 years, including the last five at Hirschi High School, where he has compiled a record of 118-94. He was an assistant at Hirschi in 1988 when the team finished second in the Texas High School 4A State Boys Basketball Tournament.

Set Plays To Isolate Key Players In Middle
By Stan Jones, Men's Assistant Coach, University Of Miami, Coral Gables, Fla.

A FACETIOUS philosophy in coaching is that to build a successful team you must get a point guard, a post player and an athlete to whom you get the ball in the middle of the floor.

Then you can play the superintendent's and banker's sons and keep your job. I am sure there are some coaching positions to which this scenario applies.

The one part of this scheme I agree with 100 percent is getting the ball isolated in the middle of the floor with your best players. According to this concept, coaches should create a series of plays to isolate matchup advantages with any player. This leads to a positive scoring opportunity in crunch times as individual matchups are studied and exploited.

POINT GUARD ISOLATION

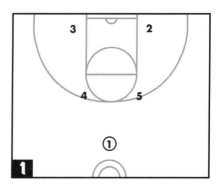

Diagram 1: Run isolation plays out of your base offensive set. In this set, the post players, 4 and 5,

start in a position where they straddle the arc of the three-point line and face the midline as wide as the lane. The wings, 2 and 3, should be positioned rim high about 5 feet off the lane. The point guard usually begins in the middle of the floor but not in all sets.

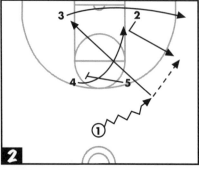

Diagram 2: Enter the ball to 2 at the wing to begin isolation. 1 splits the posts to the opposite block. 3 cuts to the ball-side corner. 5 side

screens for 4, who curls to the ball-side block.

After screening, 5 takes a position two steps higher than the original position. On the reversal pass, make sure passers lead the pass receiver to a spot. If there is intense overplay by the defense, key the backdoor pass from 2 to 4.

Diagram 3: Upon reception of the pass reversal from 5 at the top of the key, 1 has three options: catch and shoot; catch, sweep the ball under the defender and beat the defender on a drive to the basket; and catch, fake sweep, one hard dribble into the lane and shoot the pull-up jump shot.

WING ISOLATION

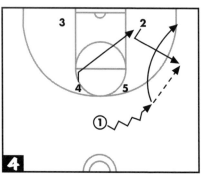

Diagram 4: Start this option with

the same wing entry pass out of the same set. On the pass, 1 will cut through the gap to the ball-side corner. 4 V-cuts and posts up on the ball-side block.

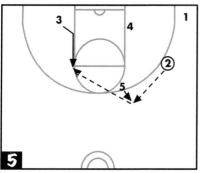

Diagram 5: After the cuts, 5 steps back for the reversal pass. 3 sets the defender and explodes to receive the ball in the same position as 1 in the previous play.

POST ISOLATION

This is a good option for any level, especially in high school where many post players could be guards. If a team has an advantage in quickness, this look is great to call.

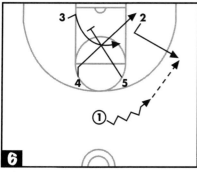

Diagram 6: For simplicity, start with the same entry pass as previously described. Opposite post V-cuts to the ball-side block. 5 diago-

nally screens for 3. 3 sets the defender up and works to get the ball.

Diagram 7: If the isolation for 3 in the post is not available, 1 regains his or her previous position after 3 has crossed the midline. 5, also in the same position as 3 and 1 in previous isolation plays, looks to explode up the lane and create the scoring opportunity.

Stan Jones has been the men's assistant coach at the University of Miami in Coral Gables, Fla., for five years. Previously, he was the boys' head coach at Jackson Academy in Jackson, Miss., for five years, during which he won two state championships and posted a record of 141-28. Jones posted an overall record of 319-89 and won four state championships on the high school level in 14 years.

COACHES have many offensive concepts to choose from to benefit their teams. A 1-4 series used to isolate post players and open shots for perimeter players is a successful method to secure scoring opportunities for key players.

PLAY 40

Diagram 1: 1 takes one or two dribbles toward the wing and makes a high-post entry pass to 5. As 5 catches the ball, 4 dives into the lane looking for a pass from 5. If the pass can't be made, 4 posts at the block.

Diagram 2: 5 passes to 3, who looks to 4 posting. 2 back screens for 5. 3 looks to throw the lob to 5.

Diagram 3: If the lob does not present itself, 3 reverses the ball to 2 or 1 for potential shots or dumps the ball down low to 5 posting up.

PLAY 41

Diagram 4: 1 passes to 2. 4 dives low and goes opposite if he or she does not receive a pass on the cut. 1 and 3 exchange.

Diagram 5: 5 ball screens for 2 and rolls to the basket.

Diagram 6: If 2 can't make a play, 2 passes to 1, who looks at 4 posting up.

PLAY 42

Diagram 7: 1 passes to 2 and shuffle cuts off 4. 2 looks to pass to 1 on the cut and the ensuing post up. 5 drops to the low post. 3 spots up in the corner.

Diagram 8: 2 passes to 4. 5 ducks into the lane. 3 V-cuts to get open on the wing.

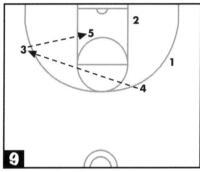

Diagram 9: If 4 is unable to pass to 5 in the lane, the pass goes to 3 on the wing. 3 looks to pass to 5 inside.

PLAY 43

Diagram 10: 1 passes to 2. 3 cuts to the low post.

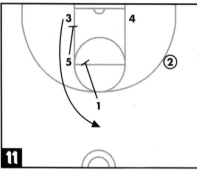

Diagram 11: 5 and 1 set a staggered double-screen for 3, who cuts out top for the possible three-point shot.

Diagram 12: If 3 is not open for the shot, 3 swings the ball to 1, who steps out from the lane and moves beyond the three-point line. 1 looks for 5 posting up.

PLAY 44

Diagram 13: 1 drives off 4's ball

screen to the wing. 2 back screens for 5, who cuts to the ball-side post.

Diagram 14: 4 down screens for 2 on the cut to the three-point line for a possible shot.

Diagram 15: If 2 does not have the open shot, the pass goes to 3, who looks at 4 posting.

Steve Smith has led Oak Hill Academy to two national championships, compiled a record of 375-29 and had 10 players drafted by National Basketball Association teams in his 13-year career.

"Go" Play For High-Percentage Shots

By David Hauser, Boys' Head Coach,
Westfield High School, Westfield, Wis.

THIS PLAY establishes good looks at high-percentage inside shots and gives solid opportunities for three-point shots. The ball must get into the paint for a pull-up jumper, a pass to a post player or a three-point shot attempt.

KEYS TO THE PLAYS

1 The player who penetrates can be 1, 2 or 3. Get the ball to the player who penetrates best or who has the best mismatch.

2 Ball must get into the lane to be effective on penetration.

3 Post players must work hard to get into position.

4 2 and 3 must be good spot-up shooters from the outside.

GO PLAY NO. 1

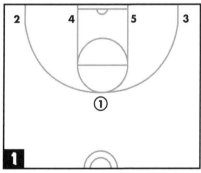

Diagram 1: 1 sets up at the top of the key or even farther out. The key is to keep the floor spread and let the players get set up.

Diagram 2: 1 penetrates as far as possible for the pass or layup. 4 and 5 move toward the post to get ready for the ball. 4 and 5 seal their defenders by stepping in front of them and moving into position to get an angle to receive a pass. The pass is usually a bounce pass from 1 to 4 or 5. 1 dribbles to one side of the lane unless the open drive down the middle of the lane for a pull-up jumper is available.

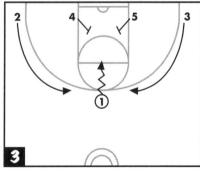

Diagram 3: While 1 is penetrating, 2 and 3 spot up for a shot. If 1 has nothing open, 2 and 3 are available for the kick-out pass and shot.

Guards are responsible to be back for the pass. 2 must spot up but not rebound.

GO PLAY NO. 2

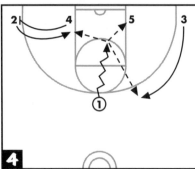

Diagram 4: Same setup as shown in Play No. 1. Once 1 has determined a side of the lane to attack, shown here as the right side, the opposite post player, 4, screens the wing, 2. 1 looks to pass to 2 coming off the screen, to 5 in the post or 3 cutting to the top of the three-point arc.

GO PLAY NO. 3

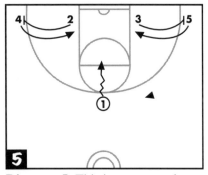

Diagram 5: This is a reverse play in which the offense is looking for a mismatch on 2 or 3. If there is no mismatch, 2 and 3 screen 4 and 5, respectively. 2 and 3 then spot up for shots. 2 must hustle to get back.

END PLAY

Diagram 6: Use this play at the end of a quarter or half for a good look at an outside shot. For a three-point shot, 1 drives and kicks out to 2 or 3 breaking from the corner to the area outside the three-point line. 2 and 3 can set up inside the three-point line and take the open jump shot. 4 and 5 crash the boards for the rebound. This can also be used as a regular set play.

David Hauser has coached boys basketball since 1992.

COACHES STRUGGLE with out-of-bounds plays every year, but a few run properly are enough against any defense. When your team must inbound from under its basket, four basic plays dramatically help if you have two to run against a man-to-man defense and two to run against a zone defense.

MAN-TO-MAN PLAYS

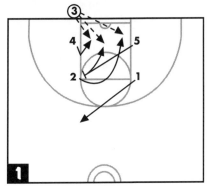

Diagram 1: This simple screen-the-screener play takes a little time to develop. 3 looks for 2, 4 or 5 coming off a screen. 1 is the release in case nothing is there. The key to the play is patience. 3 must let the screens develop.

Bruce Thomas has been a boys basketball coach for the past 12 years, eight of which he has been a head coach. In 1993, he took his former team, Cardinal Stritch High School in Oregon, Ohio, to a sectional title.

Diagram 2: This shows a screen across the lane for two big players. 5 or 4, depending on where the ball is taken out, screens across for the opposite post player and rolls back to the ball. 1 and 2 move to open areas. Patience is again the key.

ZONE PLAYS

Diagram 3: 3, your best shooter, receives a screen from 5 or 4 for the shot from the corner. After the slap of the ball, 5 breaks to the corner and 2 breaks to the wing. 3 first

looks to 5, then looks to 2. As the pass goes to 2, 5 screens down for 3, who steps in bounds toward the

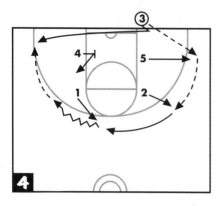

middle and pops to the corner looking for the ball. 5 posts up after screening in case the defense cheats out toward the corner. If the defense cheats, 3 passes inside to 5. 4 flashes to the high post after the pass to 3. 1 is the release.

Diagram 4: The play begins as in Diagram 3. The only difference is that after the pass to 5 in the corner, 3 receives a screen from 4 and goes opposite the pass for a shot from the corner. 5 reverses to 2. 2 reverses to 1. 1 looks to 3 in the wing area.

Out-Of-Bounds Series
By Duane Ford, Boys' and Girls' Head Coach,
Central Columbia High School, Bloomsburg, Pa.

WHEN YOU regularly face a man-to-man defense during the season, consider how many times you are forced to inbound the ball from the sideline. In such situations, you appreciate how important it is to have a scheme that allows you to inbound the ball with an opportunity to score.

In some games against extremely tough, aggressive defenses, an out-of-bounds play can be the

Duane Ford has coached boys and girls basketball for more than 25 years. He led the Central Columbia boys team to the Mid Penn Lake Conference title four of the last five years, the District 4 AA title in 1996 and the District 4 AAA title in 1997. He has accumulated more than 300 victories in his career.

equivalent of an alternate offense rather than merely a play. The concept is simple and requires only proper spacing and recognition of what is happening on the court.

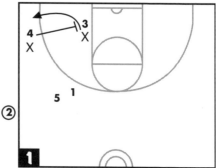

Diagram 1: Basic alignment is shown. 2 takes the ball out of bounds. Twenty feet below the ball, your best inside player is positioned near the sideline. Your

best outside shooter is positioned near the foul line. Staggered a few feet below the ball are 1 and 5.

On the slap of the ball by 2, 4 picks for 3, who pops out to the three-point line.

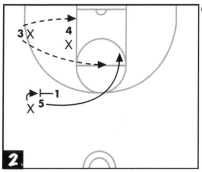

Diagram 2: If the defense switches on the pick, 3 should be open for a quick shot or a pass inside to 4 if 4's defender is sealed low. 1 picks for 5, who circles toward the basket. 1 and 5 should run this play every time the ball enters low.

Diagram 3: Any time the ball enters low, 1 should pick for 5, who then circles toward the basket. If there is a switch low and 3 can't receive the inbounds pass, 2 looks directly inside to 4 for a mismatch. 1 picks for 5 on the low entry pass.

Diagram 4: Whenever the pass can't enter low to 3 or 4, a pick and roll should be run by 5 and 1. If 1 gets the pass, 5 picks for 2, who is circling to the lane for a pass and drives to the basket or continues through the lane and moves out for a three-point shot.

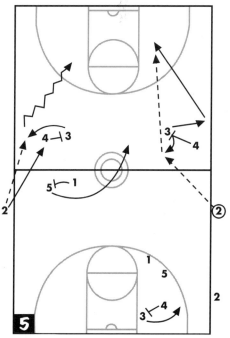

Diagram 5: If the inbounds pass must be made farther away from the basket, the spacing and align-

ments are the same as shown in these multiple formations. The operating room, however, creates other possibilities, such as a speed drive by 3 in the open court or a pass to 4 with 3 flying to the basket.

Depending on the speed, size and shooting ability of your players, other options can be devised in terms of the initial alignment. In the past, 1 has been low and 5 has taken the ball out of bounds for us with 2 and 3 positioned high.

Diagram 7: This quick-hitting option takes advantage of teams which are familiar with your offensive plays. Simply have players make the top cut first and catch the defense waiting for the low cuts.

This offense pressures and intimidates defenses by forcing them to worry about your team's ability to score quickly and easily.

Diagram 6: This variation is called "Lower," especially when the ball is moved down near the top of the key. 3 sets up inside the lane and starts moving out, but cuts quickly to the ball. After completion of the pass, 4 picks for 2, who returns for a pass from 3. 3 can opt to go one-on-one.

Glossary of Terms

(Note: Positional descriptions can vary based on players.)

Ballhandler—The player who dribbles and runs the offense.

Ball side—The side of the court where the ball is located.

Baseline—The line at either end of the court that runs parallel to the backboard. Can describe players' motion toward the baseline in offensive movement.

Block—The portion of the free-throw lane nearest the baseline.

Center—Usually the tallest player on a team.

Cutter—Player who moves off a screen toward the basket or to receive a pass.

Fast break—An offensive strategy in which a team advances the ball quickly up the court to score an easy basket.

Field goal—A successful attempt at a shot.

Forward—A player who is usually tall and can shoot from the perimeter and rebound.

Free throw—A 15-foot shot taken from the foul line.

Free-throw line—A line 15 feet from the basket behind which players take free throws.

Free-throw line extended—A parallel position extended to the right or left of the free throw line by a few feet.

Help side—Opposite the ball.

High post—The area around and near the free-throw line.

Inbounds pass—Throwing the ball in play from out of bounds.

Hook shot—Offensive set shot during which the player turns his or her body sideways and arcs a ball in the air toward the basket. Usually done by a forward or center.

Jump shot—An attempt from the floor to make a basket, usually from more than 5 feet away from the basket.

Lay up—A shot from very close range, usually as a player dribbles directly at the basket.

Low post—Area along the free-throw line.

Man-to-man—Each player is assigned the responsibility of playing against one specific player from the other team.

Out of bounds—Outside the playing area. The area from which a pass can be made to bring the ball in the area of play.

Perimeter—Outside the free-throw lane.

Pivot foot—Offensive player must keep this foot in contact with the floor at all times when not dribbling.

Point guard—Primary ballhandler in the offense.

Post—Area along the free-throw lane and halfway up the lane toward the free-throw line.

Press—When the defense extends pressure to the half-court line (half-court press), to the free-throw line (three-quarters press) or to the baseline (full-court press).

Screen—An offensive player intentionally blocks the path of a defensive player.

Screener—An offensive player who blocks the path of a teammate's defensive player.

Strong side—Side of the court where the ball is located.

Three-point line—Semicircle that runs around the perimeter of the basket and from beyond which a basket worth three points is attempted.

Three-point shot—Shot from beyond the three-point line.

Top of the key—Area slightly beyond the top of the free-throw lane.

Weakside—Area of the court opposite the ball.

Wing—Area to the side of the offensive setup, usually the free-throw line toward the sideline.

Zone—When players are assigned a certain area to play instead of a certain player to play.

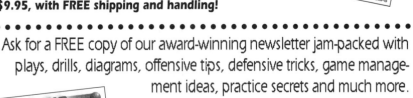